The Hitch-Hiker's Guide
to the Oceans

Have you ever seen a yacht sailing in a warm afternoon sun with all sails set and moving along in a gentle breeze? Have you wished you could be aboard destined for warmer climes populated by sun-bronzed, happy, carefree people?

Thousands of people of all ages, from all walks of life and from all countries of the world, are doing this very thing. They are known as yachties. These people are living a cruising lifestyle on a sailing boat and   visiting foreign lands. You can also experience this lifestyle by following the steps described in this book.

Whether your desire is to own a boat, or simply to sail on one, and if a life on the high seas beckons you, read on.

The Hitch-Hiker's Guide to the Oceans

Crewing around the world

Fourth edition

Alison Muir Bennett

ADLARD COLES NAUTICAL
London

Published by Adlard Coles Nautical
an imprint of A & C Black Publishers Ltd
37 Soho Square, London W1D 3QZ
www.adlardcoles.com

First published in Great Britain by Adlard Coles 1990
Second edition published by Adlard Coles Nautical 1996
Third edition 2000
Fourth edition 2003

ISBN 0-7136-6213-1

A CIP catalogue record for this book is available from the
British Library.

A & C Black uses paper produced with elemental chlorine-free pulp,
harvested from managed sustainable forests

Typeset in 10½ on 12pt Sabon by Falcon Oast Graphic Art
Printed and bound in Great Britain by The Cromwell Press,
Trowbridge, Wiltshire

Note: While all reasonable care has been taken in the publication of
this book, the author and publisher take no responsibility for the use
of the methods or products described in the book.

www.hitch-hikersguidetotheoceans.com

Contents

About the Author

Alison Muir Bennett became involved with the cruising lifestyle as a traveller rather than a sailor. Being a founder partner in an overland expedition company in the 1960s provided the opportunity to make many extended and unique journeys in the Middle East, India, Nepal, Burma and across the African continent from Europe to South Africa over a period of ten years. Then, wanting to travel in a more personal way she left the overland company to make a two year journey from USA through Central and South America to Cape Horn and back through the Caribbean. Subsequently she returned to Asia to travel for two years in India, Malaysia, Indonesia, Philippines, Thailand, China, Korea and Hawaii.

It was during this time in the Far East that, not wanting to give up travelling, but needing a new perspective of life, sailing the oceans of the world seemed to present the right combination of personal challenge, travel, and transport. Plans began to develop to go into a partnership to have a 42ft ketch built.

Realizing she did not know enough about the sea environment she spent a year taking courses in USA, UK and the Mediterranean, learning how to sail, to live aboard, and to navigate. Real cruising began when the yacht was launched in January 1981, followed by a three year voyage spending time in many remote islands and areas whilst sailing through the China Seas, Western Pacific, Bismarck, Solomon and Coral Seas, and across the Indian Ocean to South Africa.

When in South Africa Alison took the opportunity to cross the South Atlantic as crew on a friend's 42ft yacht to the Caribbean before returning to Cape Town to join her yacht partner for a voyage to Bahia, Brazil and down the coast to Buenos Aires at the end of 1989. Then, living in Brazil, there was the opportunity to enjoy some coastal sailing.

Ten years of continual yachting provided all she had hoped for, and more!

Introduction

This book aims to point out the adjustments one has to make when changing to a cruising lifestyle, and to present the necessary information to do so successfully.

It seems inappropriate in today's world to distinguish between men and women when outlining the preparatory steps and desirable skills for obtaining a crew position. In this book, we have made no such distinction. The procedures and situations described here apply to males and females alike; I know of no other environment where the traditional roles are swapped to such an extent as in the cruising world. Men are required to cook, wash, clean and sew, along with all the tasks associated with actual sailing – and anyway, often there are *only* men or *only* women on board. In mixed crews, women who happen to be fulfilling the role of cook are required to be equally handy on deck, for watches, helming, winching, sail changing and maintenance. There is no place in cruising for those people who can only cope with traditional male/female roles.

However, women can do some tasks better than men, and there are other tasks that men can accomplish with greater ease than women. It is a fundamental fact of the human species. Obviously, people will gravitate towards those skills that suit them best, but there are no prescribed roles for men and women in cruising. Adventure is a matter of personality rather than gender, age or occupation.

Having made the change, you may decide the lifestyle is not for you. If this is so, then I hope that this book will at least have helped you conduct your experiment with success. However, the step you make initially may so suit you that you will want to take further steps to continue. In which case, it is hoped that a measure of your success can be attributed to this book.

1

Definitions

To understand fully the text of this book, a few terms need to be explained. Some of these definitions are taken directly from dictionaries; those unlisted in dictionaries are the author's definitions.

Sailor: A seaman, a mariner, a member of a ship's crew.

Yacht: Fast sailing vessel, a boat propelled by sail and/or motor and used for pleasure trips, private cruising or racing. To sail, voyage or race in a yacht.

Yachtsman: One who owns or sails a yacht.

Lifestyle: Person's general pattern of living.

Mental: Pertaining to the totality of an individual's intellectual and emotional processes.

Physical: Pertaining to the body, to material nature, and the properties, processes, laws or sciences of nature.

Financial: Concerned with money matters.

For an accurate understanding of the author's text in this book, the following words should be defined as:

Sailor: A person who knows how to use the wind to make a yacht go where he or she wants.

Yachtsman: A person who uses a yacht for the sport of racing and sailing.

Yachtie: A person who uses a yacht as a home and as a means to travel.

Free lifestyle: Not in the financial sense. A stimulating, challenging lifestyle governed by nature.

Conventional lifestyle: Created and governed by man for social, political and financial desires based on the Western work ethic.

Cruising lifestyle: Living on a yacht, travelling on the sea, being in a nautical environment.

History of Yachting

A brief history of yachting seems appropriate to set the scene, including a mention of the prestigious Royal Yacht Squadron with their model-designed boats and paid crews maintained primarily for racing; these had a great impact on the evolution of yachting.

All boats, whatever size, designed for pleasure may be called yachts. The word *yacht* is originally Dutch and can be traced back to the sixteenth century in Holland. The Dutch *jacht*, short for *jachtschiff*, was a fast light sloop-rigged sailing vessel also used as a fast pirate ship, derived from the words *jacht* (vessel of state), *jagen* (hunt or chase) and *schiff* (ship), meaning hunting ship. *Mary*, a boat of this type, was presented by the Dutch nation to King Charles II of England in 1660.

Subsequently, on 1 September 1661, Charles II and his brother James, Duke of York, raced each other over 23 miles from Greenwich to Gravesend on the Thames and back. It may be said that yachting started in England from this race, called the Hundred Pound Stake Race.

Although the oldest club in the world is the Royal Cork Yacht Club of Ireland, established in 1720, and the oldest active club is the Starcross Yacht Club of Devon, whose first regatta was held in 1772, it is generally accepted that Cowes is the cradle of yachting as we know it today. From the 1770s races were recorded and in 1788 there was a race for a prize of 30 guineas. The Yacht Club was established in 1815 by forty-two yacht owners, becoming the Royal Yacht Squadron in 1833.

Cowes on the Isle of Wight, opposite the British sea port of Southampton, is the home of the Royal Yacht Squadron. Cowes Castle was built in 1540 for coastal defence by King Henry VIII, and the Royal Yacht Squadron has had its headquarters at Cowes Castle since 1856. Nearby, Osborne House became Queen

Victoria's holiday residence in 1845. Today, the annual sailing regatta of Cowes Week is an important British social event. Organized yachting in America began with the founding of the New York Yacht Club in 1844. Australia's yachting history had its starting point with the founding of the Royal Sydney Yacht Squadron in 1862. On their centenary, in 1962, they made their first challenge for the America's Cup.

In New Zealand the Auckland Yacht Club founded in 1871 became the Royal New Zealand Yacht Squadron in 1902. However, the first New Zealand challenge for the America's Cup was made in 1988 by the Mercury Bay Yacht Club.

The America's Cup, the oldest and best-known trophy in international yacht competitions, was first offered by the Royal Yacht Squadron in 1851 for a race around the Isle of Wight; it was then known as the Hundred Guinea Cup. Out of sixteen starters, the race was won by the 100-foot schooner *America*, specially built for a syndicate of New York Yacht Club owners. Consequently, the trophy became known as the America's Cup. It was presented later to the New York Yacht Club in 1857 for a perpetual international competition trophy.

Yachting or boating as a pastime that would be recognisable now did not emerge until 1845, thirty years after the founding of the Royal Yacht Squadron. The sport was initially supported and encouraged by royalty and, in a seafaring nation, official patronage naturally extended to it. During the early lifetime of the America's Cup, the contests had a great influence on yacht design, and that influence continues today. An early effect was a compromise between the conflicting ideas behind the British deep-keeled vessels and the American beamy, shallow-draft centreboards. The enormous sums spent raised the science and art of design to a level of exceptional refinement for the yachts competing for the Cup – ranging from 44 metres (143ft) to 14 metres (46ft).

After the First World War there was a boom in small boat building, partly because of the great increase in costs for vessels like the pre-war big class yachts, but also because interest in yachting was spreading and many owners now preferred sailing their own boats instead of employing professional crews.

Alongside these changes, other events were bringing about

the end of an era. In 1775 the first successful steam-driven boat was built, and even though commercial sailing vessels continued to be used and preferred for more than a hundred years after this event, sailing ships eventually disappeared from the oceans of the world with the introduction of mechanically propelled ships. The training ships used by the navies of many nations may be the last of the utilitarian sailing vessels.

The idea of using a small sailing boat for the purpose of personal adventure travel is relatively new, and scarcely predates the twentieth century. It is generally recognized that the first person to fall into the category of 'yachtie' was Joshua Slocum who, in the late 1800s, turned his professional seamanship skills, no longer in demand, towards his own requirements and pleasure.

At the age of fifty-one, and with twenty years' experience of sailing all over the world in merchant sailing ships, Slocum found himself out of work and disillusioned with prospects on land. As a consequence of this, he decided to rebuild a boat, the gift of a friend, and in 1895 he set sail on a voyage around the world in his 37-foot sloop *Spray*. The completion of his solo circumnavigation in a boat of this type brought him, his skills, and his adventure sharply to the attention of the world, setting a trend that was to be followed by others for years to come. His personal odyssey of a little over three years brought fulfilment and meaning to his life again.

In the 1940s, after the Second World War, there were various ways for individuals to acquire a boat suitable for an extended voyage for travel and pleasure. If they had the time and skill, they could build it themselves; or, if they had the means, they could have it custom built. There were boatyards building yacht designs to order, and there was also a second-hand market. By the mid-1950s the advances in modern technology, and the development of fibreglass, meant that the mass production of yachts became possible for the first time. In 1955, 4 per cent of boats were built in fibreglass; by 1970, the figure had risen to 70 per cent, promoted by the boom of Boat Shows in the 1960s.

Now that the average person had the opportunity to acquire a yacht for pleasure and travel, and yachts became available to a wider market, there evolved not only a new industry, but also an alternative lifestyle – that of a yachtie. The converging of these practical and social influences had not occurred before in the history of yachting. Previously, sailing had been the privilege of the elite at the Royal Yacht Squadron, or a military or commercial enterprise, and the ordinary person volunteered to go to sea out of poverty and necessity, or was shanghaied and press-ganged out of misfortune.

The significance of a book of this nature today is that more and more ordinary people are willingly going to sea for adventure and pleasure, and are looking for ways to accomplish a yachting lifestyle. This has become a new era in yachting history – a situation that has only come into existence since the mid-1960s, but one that will undoubtedly grow.

Racing Versus Cruising Yachts

There are two basic types of yacht: racing and cruising. And the difference is just as pronounced as when comparing the family car with the formula racing machine. The only similarity is that both have a mast and are powered by the wind. The highly technical nature of the ocean-racing yacht creates different demands on the crew, and their needs are different from those of the crew of a cruising yacht. On a racing yacht crew only live aboard for the duration of the race. This book will be dealing only with crewing on a cruising yacht.

While crewing in Mexican waters on a cruising yacht, the opportunity arose to look over the racing fleet which had just completed a race from Los Angeles, California, to Puerto Vallarta, Mexico. It is amazing how unfamiliar ocean-racing yachts look to a cruising sailor. The shape of their hulls, and the maze of electronic equipment surrounding the cockpit with multi-coloured lines running in every direction seems totally alien.

The skipper of a racing yacht is usually pushing the boat to its limit to get the fastest speed, carrying all sail possible including giant spinnakers. All this requires large crews with constant attention and helming, and much physical effort.

The cruising yacht will carry less sail for comfort, to avoid wear and tear on the boat and especially during the night for safety. Equipped with self-steering gear, the cruising yacht will, under most points of sail, steer itself; and with the introduction of self-furling sails, a smaller crew and less effort is required on deck. This is illustrated by the fact that, on a 5000-mile voyage from Australia to South Africa across the Indian Ocean over a period of five months, with three to four people aboard, it was in general only necessary to be at the helm, steering manually, while leaving and entering ports and making sail changes.

The Success Formula

It is not the purpose of this book to extol the virtues of the yachting lifestyle. Its purpose is to provide you with a plan and the relevant information and advice so that you too can participate successfully, whether it be for a short period only or a whole lifetime.

Many people – both those just completing their education and about to enter the job market, and those who have already spent a lifetime in it – think at times that they would like to escape from the pressures of the highly competitive nature of our Western society.

Life in the twentieth century has taught us that, to be successful, you must set a goal and then create a plan that will attain that goal.

The first principle of a success formula is to be aware of a need and fill it. Since there are a large number of yachts sailing the oceans of the world (no one knows exactly how many, but numbers run into the thousands), a need exists at various times and places for crew members to help the owners and/or skippers of these yachts to achieve their individual goals.

Any scientist, or expert in their field, can tell you that for a formula to become successful it must be followed precisely with no sequences left out. The personal preparation required to become an effective, sought-after crew member is:

Mental   – Understand goals
              Collect information and knowledge
Physical   – Acquire skills required
              Be aware of your own requirements and needs
Financial – Establish properly how much the enterprise will cost
              Look into the alternatives of costs
              Be efficient about carrying money and documents

Mental Preparation

Skipper/crew goals and relationships

You would think that all skippers dream of going to sea for the same reasons. However, this is not the case. There are three basic goals; a skipper may have only one or a combination of the three:

1 *Escape*
   This may be from society's pressures, man-made rules or a broken relationship
2 *Accomplishment*
   To achieve a goal or ambition, to attain something beyond one's usual efforts
3 *Pleasure*
   For the sheer excitement and enjoyment of fulfilling your own desires

It will take some investigation on your part to determine the goals of prospective skippers. In fact, skippers themselves may not be fully aware what their goals are. Also, on interviewing for a crew position, a skipper may not always reveal what his or her true feelings are; these feelings may also be modified, manipulated and presented differently according to the age and sex of the people involved.

Even though we like to think of the cruising lifestyle as an unencumbered and easygoing communal living (which it can be), it is not a democracy. The skipper has the first and last word and sets down the rules in every aspect of the conditions in which you will live. This is not to say that it cannot be enjoyable; the considerate skipper will usually consult the crew on various decisions.

It can be hard for some people to tolerate such autocratic

conditions and get used to obeying orders, especially when they are not in agreement or when the skipper seems to be unreasonable. One thing you must realize is that the skipper, no matter how easygoing he or she may be, has the final and ultimate say as to *where* and *when* you go. Consequently, your personal goals for sailing should be in tune with the skipper's, so make sure you understand what they are.

The decision as to where will be based on one of the three reasons for going to sea. If, for instance, 'accomplishment' is the reason, a trip could be planned to venture into the high latitudes, possibly around 'the Horn' and possibly against prevailing winds, so as to achieve a full measure of accomplishment.

At the opposite end of the scale, if pleasure is the consideration, the skipper would stay in the mid-latitudes, preferably between 20°N and 20°S, where the pleasant prevailing trade winds blow from east to west.

The escapist will probably be tempted to go to the more remote areas where living conditions will be very basic, but extremely interesting. Some may wish only to remain at sea as much as possible. It should be realized, though, that people cannot truly escape from personal problems, for they will bring them along wherever they go.

All these categories will contain their own type of adventures – like it or not!

The most successful voyage is the one that, in one's mind's eye, has already been completed before departure. Since it is desirable to provide the prospective crew member with as much information as possible on the true conditions and experiences that they may be confronted with, it becomes necessary to discuss some of the negative aspects as well as the positive. Forewarned is forearmed.

All too often a yacht owner or skipper new to the cruising lifestyle will spend all his or her time and energy on the acquisition of the yacht and its preparation for sea, and have time for few, if any, thoughts about his or her feelings and attitudes. Even some experienced skippers can become so preoccupied with the requirements of the yacht when preparing for extensive cruising that they overlook their own feelings and those of the crew. This, more often than we like to think, can have serious consequences. On a voyage with the pressures of command in the ever-changing and unknown world at sea, in some extremes of emotional and mental conflict between skipper and crew, death has occurred. Such a tragedy can evolve from powerplay, jealousies, and in general a skipper who cannot cope; and the best advice is not to go to sea with an inexperienced skipper. The only exception to this rule would be a person who you feel you know very well, and in whose ability to perform under stress you have absolute confidence. When skippers have previous experience there is still no real way of knowing how well they can cope until you are at sea. Even though they may be technically adept they may not have the ability to handle people.

Too many times stories are heard of 'hell ships' on ocean passages, and crew jumping ship at the first port, or crew members being told unceremoniously to get off the boat. As a rule, the boat will survive the journey easily; it is the people who become the casualties.

It is worth mentioning that sometimes problems arise as a result of personality changes at sea, and this is equally applicable to skipper or crew. The eager helper on shore can become a very reluctant deckhand, the seemingly orderly person a slob, or the reasonable fellow a tyrant. This is partly due to the fact that simple, ordinary everyday tasks on land take on a different importance and aspect, and even become difficult and dangerous when in a boat. The routine of life at sea alters normal activities like eating, sleeping and relaxing, due to watches and the progress of the boat, and, if these activities are not properly organized and carried out, they can lead to conflict.

The skipper who knows, and is willing to admit to, his or her physical or mental weaknesses will sign on as crew a person who is capable in those particular areas. After all, we are all imperfect human beings and as such all have shortcomings. A good, confident skipper need not be superhuman, but one who is aware and is flexible in responding to his or her own and others' feelings and needs. This does not mean accommodating everyone's idiosyncrasies, but simply being aware of them can help. The experience of cruising can then be happy and fulfilling, not necessarily because of the compatibility of the people involved, but in spite of the differences.

A crew member must also take into account that the whole matter of owning a boat is 90 per cent emotional, and that not to show due respect for a skipper's boat, home and equipment will cause very adverse reactions. Anyone who owns their own weekend sailing boat but dreams of greater voyages will appreciate this point.

Considering the name of the yacht can be a real insight into the psychology of a skipper. The names indicate variously: humour, practicality, challenge, inspiration, aggressiveness, sentimentality, love, romance, partnerships, display, ego, origins and superstitions. If it is not apparent to you, ask the skipper the meaning or significance of the yacht's name to them.

Here are a few examples for you to consider:

Thrasher	Laughing Water
Freebooter	Magic Adventurer
Banshee	Enchantress
Vagabond	Wanderer
Force 8	Morning Mist
Galeforce	Gentle Rush
Spirit of Eskimo Nell	Wave Maiden
Hot Lips	Mary Ann
Hotspur	Lady of Larne

If the name has been inherited ask the skipper what name they would have chosen. Would they consider changing the name? It is supposed to be unlucky, is that a consideration? You'd be surprised how much you can learn from this topic of conversation!

Travelling by crewing on yachts should not be considered as just a cheap form of travel. Instead, you should see it as an opportunity to share someone's home and yacht for an experience that you might not otherwise be able to have. Skippers are generally looking for someone who wants to participate and share in every aspect of shipboard life both in port and at sea. Whatever financial arrangements you have with the skipper for the intended voyage, remember it is not simply a travel ticket; there is a commitment to the skipper as a crew member for the agreed period of time, or destination, and the agreement should be honoured.

Look for a skipper who is open and willing to talk about all areas of the cruising life: mental, physical and financial.

Sailing as a couple

Sailing as a couple could alter the whole course of your relationship! There are several ways in which you could find yourself sailing with another person who is close to you:

Crewing **for** your lover/spouse
Crewing **with** your lover/spouse
A shipboard romance
Crewing with a friend
Crewing with couples

What we shall discuss here is not necessarily what will happen inevitably, but what has been observed to happen to some people. You could be taken unpleasantly by surprise if you are not prepared for a possible change of balance within the relationship under these particular circumstances.

Crewing for your lover/spouse

In the introduction it seemed important to point out that the traditional male/female roles are swapped around a great deal amongst a crew at sea. If you are crewing for your lover this will still be the case, but with a difference. The difference arises not only out of your particular kind of relationship but because one of you will be the 'skipper' and one of you will be 'crew' depending not just on the dominant person in the relationship itself, but on one person being a more experienced sailor than the other. If in normal life you have what seems to be a partnership of equality or a balanced force of personalities, you may be surprised to find yourself put into a subordinate position dealing with a torrent of commands, demands and orders, changing the whole mood and style of your life together – which you will learn to accept – or not!

Perhaps you are going to crew for your boyfriend on his yacht. You may or may not have actually lived together, but presumably you are considering this step because you have a good loving relationship where few harsh words are spoken and you feel important in his life. Voyaging on *his* yacht you may find it difficult to accept your new role. You could well become of secondary importance to the boat or anything that requires attention on it. The yacht comes first. It is valuable, and the functions of its equipment are vital to safety at sea. The yacht will demand the attention of both of you. And it may hold the attention of your lover more than any other sort of rival relationship could, leaving little time for your romance.

You will inevitably be shouted at a lot. Unfortunately in the activity of sailing it is often necessary for the skipper to shout. Perhaps to get instructions heard from helm to forepeak or vice versa, or to get a sense of urgency instilled into a manoeuvre, or to alert you to come up on deck – and to be heard over the sound of wind, sea and sail – whatever. Even though you realise that it is not necessarily because of you that you are being shouted at, but because of the circumstances, it is nevertheless *you* who are being shouted at. You may become the scapegoat for everything that goes wrong!

A woman admitted that when she was at the helm, or sunbathing bare-breasted she had learned always to keep a top handy to put on quickly in case her skipper decided on a tack or sail change, because she just could not tolerate him shouting out instructions at her when her breasts were bare. It made her feel far too vulnerable.

As shouting is an aggressive form of communication it can create a very uncomfortable, upsetting and exhausting feeling within a relationship – so beware!

This can equally be the case if you are the boyfriend of an accomplished yachtswoman. One instance comes to mind where a man, having won the heart of a woman with her own boat, was invited to sail across the Indian Ocean. On arrival in India she decided he must leave. During the voyage he discovered that he did not like taking the orders from her and tried to manoeuvre the control of the yacht from her in order to rebalance the relationship in his favour as dominant male. For her, as is usual for a yacht owner, the boat came first – and she sailed on without him.

However, at the moment this is statistically a far less common situation, and it is more likely that as a man you could be invited to crew on the yacht of your girlfriend's father. In that case you and your relationship with your girlfriend are going to be under observation a great deal – which could be an ordeal! And, you will be required to do as he says, how and when he says, which your ego may be able to accept – or not! You had better be as sure as you can that you have a genuine liking and respect for him, or else it won't work, despite what you may feel about his daughter. Within your relationship she will invariably have to respect her father's wishes as the skipper's wishes first. Your desires and plans will be secondary. This may not be made to seem obvious, but invariably it is so.

There is another aspect for a couple to consider. As a husband and wife you may have maintained home, cars, jobs, children together but you have in fact lived separate lives with your own departments, coming together at the end of the day and at weekends. Whereas on a yacht you are working together all the time, which some couples can find difficult to adapt to. Especially when the woman was probably used to making all the domestic and social decisions of everyday life as she saw fit without having to refer to anyone, and as it suited her best. It will not be the same for her at sea, she could find herself irritated by being told what to cook and when, or frustrated by not being allowed to keep certain things in particular lockers, and so on. In the house her husband would have been happy to let her get on with it, but on a yacht everything is intimately tied up with the yacht and its progress at sea. As a result it becomes his decision as well.

When you are living on a yacht together it becomes job, home, car, workshop and garden rolled into one, and areas of control overlap and invade traditional territories, which can cause some strife in a husband and wife team. There are quite a few wives who eventually abandon the yacht along with their husband saying 'let them get on with it' out of exasperation. It won't be long before somebody else finds it easier to adapt to her situation than she did.

People find their relationships being altered in many ways by the change of environment. Here is another real life example. A married couple in their thirties sailing around the world together, both of them exceptionally well experienced and equally so. They both had Master's certificates and either of them could sail the yacht perfectly well alone. The woman accidentally became pregnant, and fairly late in the pregnancy her husband succumbed to a serious tropical fever which did not manifest itself until they were a week or so into an ocean crossing. As there was no way of her knowing how serious the fever was to be, that he would actually be critically ill, unconscious, delirious, and unable to assist in any way, she decided to continue. Unassisted and heavily pregnant she arrived at their Pacific island destination in time to have the baby delivered. After this event and her husband's full recovery they continued and she was shocked to find herself relegated totally to the care of the baby. Her husband would not consider co-operating with the care of the child, and she could not come to terms with the situation as she was there to sail, and to enjoy sailing too. Consequently there were bitter arguments and the couple parted company about a year later, as soon as it was convenient during their journey, and that was the end of their sailing life together.

Crewing with *your lover/spouse*

It is a nice idea to be able to sail away together crewing in an adventure on a yacht bound on an interesting voyage. On the other hand it may be hard to have any sort of private life together on board due to watch routines or lack of a private cabin to yourselves. You may have to resort to using hotel rooms every time you arrive in port for a little private time together. Of course the skipper may not like this because it will upset his plans for maintenance work that should be done in port. Travelling as a couple you must choose your yacht carefully for its type of accommodation and routines. And how about the skipper? Does he or she have a companion? If not, why not? Has his relationship just broken up? Is he happily or reluctantly leaving his wife or girlfriend behind? Is he going to be lonely or jealous? If he has a partner how well do they get on together? Is he a committed 'loner' and will he be unsympathetic to your requirements? Or, will the woman, who might not have been attracted to the owner of the boat in a land-based situation, come to the decision that, in his role of skipper with overall control and dominance at sea, she is better off being the owner's companion rather than the crew's partner? Or vice versa!

Generally couples are quite popular as a crew because they seem to represent a package deal to a skipper, ie cook/cleaner and deckmonkey/'gofer'. If you can find the right situation it is a good way to have time together on an adventure you can share without the expense and responsibility of having your own vessel.

A shipboard romance

Many a romance blossoms at sea, at anchorages and in ports. It could be with someone on the yacht you are sailing on, or on another yacht voyaging the same way on much the same schedule. Reunions in ports are charged with extra anticipation and as a result there can be some crew swapping between yachts, which, needless to say, requires the co-operation of the skippers involved. People meet locals at the yacht clubs and marinas visited. Usually these affairs are based on the anticipation of an imminent farewell, unless a person's mind can be changed to stay behind or join the yacht – and it often is.

As many love affairs die as those that blossom at sea, and as many marriages occur as those that founder. Affairs of the heart are adequately fanned by a sea breeze it seems, one way or the other – unwanted 'crew' can be the result. It is often overlooked by women on 'the Pill' that vomiting caused by sea-sickness significantly reduces its efficiency, and alternatives are not always at hand mid-ocean. It is as well to be aware of this as a pregnancy on a sea voyage can be very inconvenient.

Crewing with a friend
When men or women who are friends decide to take off together for mutual support the friendship can be seriously taxed before ever setting sail. It often happens that a skipper will only want one of you, or only one of you is right and they'd rather choose someone else instead of your friend – maybe you don't represent the same kind of 'package deal' as a couple does. Would you go anyway and leave your friend to find some other solution? Would you decide that it's got to be for both of you or not at all? Would you be resentful of a lost opportunity? Just how keen are you to do this with or without your friend now that you have a crew position and they haven't? Whatever the outcome it could possibly be the end of a beautiful friendship unless you make some kind of agreement between you in the event of one person being chosen over another. Even if it is just understanding that this could happen.

On board it will be easier for friends than for a couple. You won't need the same sort of time together and privacy. From the start there will be at least one person you know well and can go places with in port. So if you are concerned about sailing with strangers, crewing with a friend is reassuring.

Whether you are sailing with friends, lovers, or strangers compatibility is always essential on a yacht, and sailing with lovers, and friends to a lesser degree, can introduce the compli-cations of jealousies. This deserves some consideration as jealousy is hard enough to cope with on dry land, never mind in the rarefied atmosphere at sea.

Crewing with couples

Finally, if you think that none of this will really affect you because you are travelling alone, think again. A lot of crew situations that are available are with couples, and in that little world on board a yacht you will be very much affected by the quality of the couple's relationship, in every respect.

Try to observe how they interact with each other. Do they discuss the things that must be done together? Or does one boss the other about? Do they work well together? Have they made a voyage together before?

There are two instances within two months of each other when young men set off with different couples from England and only made it as far as Europe on a voyage to the Caribbean. Both groups had chosen to leave England at a bad time of year and as a result the yachts suffered bad weather, up to Force 7, crossing the Channel – an unfortunate start for a crew new to working together. In both instances the young man abandoned his voyage to the Caribbean before leaving the Continent because he had lost confidence and respect for the skipper. The prime reason was that neither could tolerate the way in which the skipper shouted at his girlfriend all the time, particularly under difficult circumstances.

They decided it was best to cut their losses and try again. For one of them it meant waiting for another year and sailing out from the Canary Islands. The other one decided to fly to the Caribbean and try his chances there for the season, sailing back if possible.

Remember that some people undergo a character change at sea. Research the best time of year to leave. And keep in mind what will be discussed under 'Nudity'.

Socio-cultural issues

There are certain human habits and preferences in life that we do not all necessarily share. In order to identify and choose a situation that suits you personally, you should consider certain issues. On a small boat, with its limited space and close contact with other people, these things can become explosive issues, and need to be thought about in advance by both skipper and crew.

The following areas need special consideration:

Drinking	Water	Domestic chores
Smoking	Children	Music
Vegetarianism	Nudity	Boat etiquette
Drugs	Animals	Yacht club etiquette

Drinking

Some boats are 'dry'. This means that the skipper will not allow alcohol on the boat at any time, so your drinking will be confined to the periods you are ashore, or visiting other boats.

Other boats are 'dry' only at sea. The skipper will allow alcohol on board, but will restrict its consumption to the times when you are at anchor, or in port.

Yet other skippers will carry alcohol and will not mind drinking at sea within reason, such as at a 'happy hour' or with meals, when conditions allow.

And some skippers are alcoholics!

There are a number of reasons for a 'dry' boat or a 'wet' boat, stemming from strong and unchangeable convictions, from personal preferences, for reasons of safety, and for the practical problem of stowage space. However, there is no doubt that cockpit get-togethers, parties and general socializing when yachties meet in various anchorages, are the times when drinking occurs, and it is generally accepted on board.

Smoking

Some skippers will not allow smoking on board. Other skippers will allow smoking, but only on deck. And yet other skippers are chain-smokers.

The reasons here stem mostly from personal habits. There are a few things worth pointing out about smoking, even if you are on a boat which suits your personal preference as a smoker. If you are smoking on deck the skipper will not like you flicking your ash and matches all around the decks, and certainly not over the side into the dinghy which may be lying alongside! So ask what the routine is for disposing of ash and butts. Remember to discover the skipper's preferences when visiting any other boats.

If you are a non-smoker, remember that there are added hazards to living with smokers at sea. The odour can trigger off seasickness and, in windy conditions at anchor, as well as at sea, the smoke and ashes will fly around in the air and inevitably come your way.

Vegetarianism

There are people who choose to be vegetarian for religious reasons, and there are people for whom vegetarianism is a religion in itself. You will find quite a lot of yachties are vegetarians, often because they feel it's part of a healthier lifestyle. Many people living on boats find themselves, through limited availability of decent meat protein and the problems of storage and refrigeration, eating an increasingly vegetarian diet, which they will alter as and when they can. If you have a special dietary requirement you should make it known at the outset. Thus, vegetarianism really falls into two categories at sea: through choice, and by force of circumstances.

Drugs

This is a difficult subject. Some skippers even search the crew prior to leaving port, in order to be able to protect themselves according to the law. Drugs are too important an issue to be left to chance.

A skipper is responsible for any drugs of any sort on board, medicinal or recreational, and so will insist on being aware of what you have. If you are taking special medication, your skipper will need to know for the safety of your own health, and possibly the need to apply it in an emergency, as well as for the safekeeping of prescription medicines which may be on the restricted list in some countries and would therefore be of concern to Customs and Excise officers. The crew must respect the skipper's views as law!

All countries take a very hard line on recreational drugs, and having them on board could result in all, or a combination of, the following: confiscation of the boat, arrest of the skipper and crew, a long and miserable sentence, and (outside the USA and Europe) a high risk of death sentence.

Water

Don't misuse fresh water. The drinking water that can be carried on board is limited and precious and could become a matter of life and death. There can be serious social repercussions between people when someone is suspected of making wrong use of it.

Cleanliness is also very important, so you must get used to using salt water for all washing and cleaning.

Children

Be absolutely sure that you can tolerate young children and all the demands they make on life in general, if you are considering sailing on a yacht that will have them on board.

Nudity

Some people are shocked by nudity. If you are, it is as well to realize that the majority of yachties are nudists, to a greater or lesser degree.

Rather like vegetarianism, nudism can be something of a cult, or something that just occurs because of your lifestyle. With regard to the latter, you will find that a lot of people living on boats will, while at sea, 'forget' about clothes. This is not the result of any kind of exhibitionism, but it really is not necessary in the middle of an unpopulated ocean to worry about being clothed if the weather is suitable, and you like the feel of the sun and wind on your body. You save a lot of effort and inconvenience when it comes to laundering clothes, taking into consideration the shortage of fresh water. Also, it is more than likely that showering will take place out on deck.

If there is an emergency at night and it's all hands on deck, the skipper will probably come flying up out of the bunk with no clothes on to take care of the situation, and clothes will be the last thing on his or her mind, so it's best to be at ease about nudity. The time taken by crew members to make themselves 'respectable' for the job won't be appreciated either. (Foul weather gear is another matter.)

Some people cannot go without clothes simply because their complexion will not tolerate exposure to sun and wind; if this is your problem, be prepared with loose, lightweight shirts and trousers. Serious consideration should be given to the problems of skin cancer associated with over-exposure to the sun. At sea, the risk is amplified by reflection from the water.

Another matter to consider is that some couples on boats find it hard to tolerate another person of either sex being nude in the close confines of a boat. If you like to sunbathe nude ask if there is any objection first in case one half of a couple may object to nudity in a person of the opposite sex to their partner.

Although it is hardly expected that people will continue to be so casual about not wearing clothes when within sight of people on shore, it is important to remember that tolerance of the type experienced on the Côte d'Azur doesn't apply in all places. Indeed, nudity is a social offence in many cultures, even on remote islands.

Animals

Some skippers have animals they love and will not leave behind, some animals are acquired en route as visitors and others may arrive as gifts. They may be cats, dogs, monkeys, birds and so on. To many solo skippers they are their sole companions.

Apart from the fact that some people are allergic to animals, the major problem with animals on a boat is their bodily functions. Cats are probably less of a problem since they can be trained to use a litter box, but even they can find the need to re-establish their territorial limits – and your bunk may be included! It may also be that the ship's cat consistently chooses your bunk to sleep on and will eventually make it its own. Dogs are a far greater deck problem and *somebody* has to clean the decks. Both cats and dogs shed hairs, and cleanliness and odours can be a problem, especially if the weather is bad and both the animals and their boxes are confined below decks. The odour can contribute to seasickness. Also, both cats and dogs can be seasick.

Animals have to be fed and taken into consideration in daily routines. Yachts with animals on board are usually required to anchor further out than usual due to quarantine regulations and this can be a disadvantage when rowing back and forth from yacht to shore.

Another factor to consider is that some skippers take dogs for security purposes. Guard dogs on board yachts in harbours or anchorages have been known to bark continually from their owner's departure to the shore until their owner's return to the yacht.

These points are mentioned mostly for the sake of people who are not used to or interested in pets, but even if you are normally an animal lover these considerations are worth bearing in mind.

Domestic chores

Team living, whether two people are involved or more, has to be organized at sea. When dreaming of travel and sailing to far-away places, it is easy to overlook the fact that even on an adventure, mundane necessities of life have to be catered for.

Everybody is involved with cooking meals, washing up, cleaning the galley, the icebox, keeping the heads clean and hygienic, cleaning floors, etc. The skipper should see to it that these duties are carried out properly, or else the yacht will become smelly and infested with cockroaches and other creatures, and the health and morale of the crew will suffer.

Unfortunately we don't leave the tedium of domestic chores behind us when we leave land-based living. These essentials of daily life must still be carried out, and the boat's equipment should include the items necessary to keep the yacht shipshape.

Music

If you are used to listening to music all day, remember it's not possible on a yacht. The sound power would need to come from the boat's batteries and they have more important functions than being used up on light entertainment, so it's usual to get permission to use sound equipment.

Most yachts have some sort of sound system on board, usually for cassettes. With this benefit comes the problem of differences in musical tastes, and it's not always easy to be tolerant – especially if it's 'heavy metal' versus 'classical'. If you are considering taking some of your cassettes with you, find out if they are acceptable, or take a personal stereo; this way, you won't disturb anybody else.

It is also nice to have a personal stereo for entertainment during night watches. However, some skippers may not agree with crew members wearing headphones on watch, as one would not be as alert to sounds that may be important indicators of trouble on deck or danger. They can also be a hindrance to communication.

Boat etiquette

Probably one of the most important things to remember in the yachting circle is that you never get on anybody's boat without the permission or the invitation to do so. It is an unwritten rule that you always ask for 'Permission to come aboard?' from the skipper, even though you may have been on the vessel many times before – and *most* definitely if you have never been on the boat, whether you know the skipper or not. Even when you have already been invited to visit, it is the common courtesy of yachties to call out 'Permission to come aboard?' when alongside the yacht. Failure to do so is quite a serious social *faux pas*.

When you are a crew member, don't invite people on board without asking the skipper's permission to do so.

Hand in hand with this comes the tradition of never walking on a boat's deck with your shoes on. It is not polite; it is in fact rude, and it is also damaging and dirtying to the surface of the deck. It is a barefoot culture because of the lifestyle, but much more importantly because of respect for the yacht.

To overlook these aspects of etiquette will automatically make you unwelcome.

Yacht Club etiquette

Permission is also required to make use of the visiting privileges extended by most yacht clubs. You don't automatically have the right to enter a club of which you are not a member just because you are visiting on a yacht. So, sign the Visitor's Book first, if you can't find it ask for it. Introduce yourself to the Secretary and ask what is required by members for you to benefit from the facilities. Maybe a temporary membership is involved.

Some clubs are quite formal, others are very easy-going. A visiting yacht and it's crew are usually very welcome, but do go through the proper procedures first to ensure that the welcome to visitors continues.

Flag etiquette

This is a sensitive area where good practice and good manners should be followed carefully. The skipper should be aware of how, where, and when to follow protocol so be sure you have correct instructions as the procedure is based on maritime law and you don't want to get your skipper into trouble.

Very simple guidelines are:

•The flag of the country the yacht is registered in is their Ensign. British yachts 'wear' the Red Ensign prominently displayed aft.
• The Ensign is the senior flag.
• Ensigns are displayed in sight of land or other ships; raised in the morning and lowered in the evening.

- Courtesy flags are a smaller version of the normal maritime flag or Ensign of the country you are visiting.
- Courtesy flags take the second most senior position; this is the starboard crosstree/spreaders of the mast.
- A Courtesy flag must not be flown in an inferior position to any flag other than the Ensign.
- Courtesy and Quarantine flag/Q flags are signal flags.
- Signal flags are flown at the starboard crosstree/spreaders of the mast.
- The Quarantine flag is a signal for 'free practique', customs and immigrations clearance.
- The Q flag should be flown below the courtesy flag.
- Yacht club burgees should be flown from the masthead as no flag should be flown above a burgee.

For more information see the RYA website or contact the Cruising Association, details page 93.

Yachtie versus conventional lifestyle

The questions most asked of people who are cruising are: 'How did you get into cruising?' 'Do you catch fish?' 'What do you do at night?' 'Are you ever frightened?' and 'Don't you get bored?'

These things are so taken for granted by yachties that the questions seem amusing, even a little stupid. However, even these simple questions arising out of curiosity begin to show us the contrasts between the yachting lifestyle and the conventional lifestyle. The situations that are known and familiar to cruising people often seem to be puzzling aspects of life at sea to people who live on land, and these are the differences between the known and taken for granted in a life on land versus what is taken for granted in a life at sea.

In effect, people who decide to go cruising are exchanging one set of rules for another. So we are not exactly talking about a carefree holiday; there are still responsibilities, albeit different ones, in this pipe dream. It is a complete change in the pattern of one's life.

Most obvious is the 24-hour day that sailors live. The routine of watches between crew members to man the boat constantly means having to sleep at unusual times for unusual periods of time, eating meals to suit watch routines rather than at conventional meal times. Day and night are divided by sunset and dawn; one can't rely on the use of electric light on board. Power must be conserved for navigational lights and instruments, and additionally, light shining out of the boat's interior creates a night blindness effect for people on watch. Most skippers will not allow lights at night, so reading, relaxing and eating at night may no longer be possible at sea.

Fresh water is a valuable commodity at sea and people who are not used to living afloat often don't realize that it should be reserved for drinking purposes only. The boat is limited in the amount of water it can carry and this has to last the duration of the voyage. In open seas, salt water can be used for cooking and washing pots and pans, clothes and bodies. Even in some ports water is hard to obtain – and sometimes it is not available at all, or it has to be bought. In many cases it will be inconvenient to get water from shore to the yacht – somebody will have to take the dinghy ashore with 25-litre containers to replenish the supplies. If you need to use fresh water for any purpose other than drinking, you must ask the skipper first. Sometimes a yacht can carry enough fresh water for people to rinse sea water out of their hair or off their bodies.

Work and relaxation are bound together on a boat; it is not like a job to which one comes and goes at specific times with a separated workplace and home, and usually there is no pay for the duties performed.

Into this comes the contrast in the pace of life aboard; the time in which things are accomplished, the schedules of leaving and arriving. These become unknown factors at sea and can only be estimated. Most of us are used to the concept of jumping into a car to drive for a known period of time to arrive at a destination at the time we expect to. Or taking the 9.05 train which will arrive at 9.50; or, on a larger scale, knowing exactly how long it will take a plane to fly across continents and oceans and being confident it will land according to schedule.

At sea you may plan to leave on Wednesday but find that the weather conditions may not permit it for another one or two days, or even a week. In contrast, you may have to deal with an urgent departure earlier than planned; in this instance, you must be able to think quickly and efficiently under pressure, knowing exactly what has to be accomplished. You may estimate that a voyage may take ten days, but you really won't know until you get there. Maybe it will take a week, maybe ten days, maybe more – there can be no schedule. It may be of interest to note that, in general, about 60 per cent of a voyage is time spent at anchor and about 40 per cent actually sailing.

In our society of high mobility, the mode of travel by sail is, by comparison, medieval, and so are the means of communication. You can forget the days of just picking up the telephone at your side and dialling a number for instant contact, or knowing a letter will be received within a couple of days. A simple telephone call becomes a complicated exercise: getting from your anchorage to shore, finding transport into a town, going to a special international telephone call building to place a call at a certain time, having the right currency to pay (collect or reverse charge calls are not always possible). News by letter may be a month old or more by the time you receive it, and family and friends should be warned of this to reduce unnecessary panicking.

You will find that, as you are now in a boat society, mobility on shore becomes a problem, especially in the remoter places. Buses are scarce, if not non-existent, and taxis are expensive. Maybe you will be lucky enough to have a bike on board, but mostly you'll rely on your own two feet or anyone kind enough to give you a ride. Gone are the days of jumping into a car and going where and when you want.

These are the more practical contrasts; other differences fall into the category of different values of life. Things that are often important in our conventional materialistic society are fashion, the type of car we drive and the size of house we live in – the 'stage props' we use to present the desired image of ourselves to the world. The importance of all of these fades as other things grow in significance. This is not to say that these things are not carried over to a degree, but a yachtie will be much more interested in a person's personality than in material trappings. Fashion and jewellery become out of place, and clothes, when necessary, are an essential item rather than a decoration. The simple and natural things bring unexpected pleasure, like the first cold beer in a month, a breathtaking starry night, or a visit by a school of dolphins. There is no real competitiveness between yachties about the biggest, most costly boat in the harbour. Yachties are appreciative of each other's boats, large or small, custom-built, factory-built, or home-made.

The yachtie lives in a mobile community; the neighbourhood and neighbours are changing all the time, but there is always a great camaraderie between yachties. They all know why they are there, albeit for their different reasons, and they all appreciate the steps that have been taken to get there. Despite the growing number of yachts on the cruising circuit, the number of people leading this lifestyle is still a very small percentage in comparison with the world's population. For this reason, the cruising community is still unique, the characters that make it up are usually exceptional and interesting, be they good or bad, and they come from all walks of life, with all sizes and types of boats and bank balances, and all nationalities. A condensed community out of the world community.

They have decided to change their lifestyle, for whatever period of time they can, not because a conventional lifestyle is disapproved of, but because there is an alternative lifestyle available to those who wish to experience it. It is, of course, because of the very existence of our materialistic world that we now have the opportunity to take a different kind of advantage of the scientific progress and wealth it creates, and be able to experience this contrasting lifestyle.

Time sense of time world

In the cruising world there are people who set themselves the goal of a voyage within a fixed time. Some keep to their plan and are happy with it. Others who set out with the same goals find themselves slipping into a different time sense, the journey altering to suit their interests and pace until the voyage has become three or four times longer than originally planned.

Time is relative to one's frame of mind. Either in slowing down or speeding up your sense of time, to be content in your time world you should not project your thinking beyond your physical ability or desire to move, or to achieve things. The physical time we have in which to live and accomplish objectives is controlled by natural and artificial influences, or dictated by the force and rhythms of nature. If the physical conditions change you must try to be flexible enough in your thinking to adjust to the changes. The setting of goals and the resulting success of attaining them is an accomplishment people often fail to achieve because they try to control the time, or set unrealistic times, in which their goals can be realized. It is said by some that it is not the achieving of goals that brings pleasure, but the process itself. Others achieve their goals against the odds but have gone through hell to get there.

There are two types of sailor at opposite ends of the scale. On completion of a long ocean passage, one type is reluctant to go ashore on arriving in port, not wishing to leave their private 'cocoon' or wanting to deal with the hustle of the everyday world.

The other type is the sailor who has not been able to adjust his or her mental time sense to suit the natural influences while at sea; and instead of being in tune they have been at odds, or done battle with the seas whatever the conditions have been. Consequently, when arriving in port after a long sea voyage, such sailors cannot get to shore quickly enough to satisfy their sense of time and pace, and to reconnect with the world.

The first type would come from the 'escapist' category, preferring to avoid the Western lifestyle. The second type are from the 'accomplishment' category, not so much interested in changing a lifestyle as in providing themselves with continual and demanding challenges.

If somewhere between these two ends of the scale you can allow yourself to adjust and enjoy the rhythms of nature, the lulls and the challenges as they present themselves in the cruising life, there can be very real benefits resulting in a more relaxed, tension-free attitude, enhancing your health and outlook.

Paranormal Experiences

'Stranger things have happened at sea!' So goes an old saying, and it is supported by many strange stories that have been told throughout the ages. Ships disappearing without trace, abandoned ships sailing on and discovered with no trace of crew, ghost ships, extraordinary events in the so called 'Bermuda Triangle', miracles performed in answer to supplications during storms and so on. There is a rich history of stories surrounding 'happenings' at sea, and today similar stories are still being told.

There are aspects of sailing, particularly at night, which can allow an imagination to run riot. For instance, when a yacht is sailing it makes noises, sounds which initially you will find unusual. The hull can creak, groan and hum; there are rattles here and there, water swishing against the hull and sometimes crashing waves. Ropes sliding and slapping, sails fluttering and the wind singing or howling in the rigging. Even in a harbour there is the sound of the anchor chain tugging or the mooring lines straining; the crackling noise small creatures make on the hull, and the clanging of halyards on masts.

On silent nights isolated sounds like a nearby dolphin suddenly blowing air can be really startling and unnerving, or a flying fish hitting your body or thudding on the deck or into a sail can give you a fright. Sometimes there is an eerie feeling that there is someone or something else on the boat with you when you hear soft breathing sounds from the wind, and you are forever looking over your shoulder to see what is there. Some people's imagination is so strong that they are convinced they actually see strangers on board, or at least hear their conversation, and perhaps they do! One can become apprehensive at night watching what seems to be some type of UFO moving across the sky. It is probably a meteorite or one of the thousands of satellites that now revolve around the earth, but is it? And, if there is a situation in which you are very worried or nervous, perhaps when things go wrong or there is bad weather, you might suddenly find yourself with religious or superstitious feelings that lead you to invoke God, or his Mother or your own mother and to make bargains in prayers to them just like sailors long ago.

It is accepted that it is not unusual for all these things to play on the imagination and the brain to turn them into supernatural events, and it is as well to consider that some of these events may have been realities.

Conclusion

To complete this phase of mental preparation, you should read other people's accounts of their voyages – such as those of Slocum, the Smeetons, the Roths, the Hiscocks and others.

The happiest and most pleasant experience will be the one with the least amount of unpleasant surprises.

Set a goal, and create a plan of action based on the type of yacht, destination and time available. *Live* with the plan, *mentally commit* yourself to it, and have *confidence* that it will work.

Physical Preparation

Desirable skills

The person who has not sailed or experienced the cruising life would probably think the main skill required to be a desired crew member would be seamanship. This is not the case; a skipper who owns a boat and has already sailed many sea miles knows seamanship. He will prefer to teach crew members his own rules of seamanship. Make sure your skipper instructs you properly on all aspects of the boat and its equipment; in particular, safety equipment, life jackets, harnesses, radio, phone, extinguishers, pumps.

To become an accomplished sailor is an ongoing process. The old salts who have spent many years sailing the oceans are the first to admit that no two voyages are the same, and each has its lesson to be experienced and learned.

Someone who has a strong desire to go to sea and is willing to learn, knows port from starboard, how to tie a bowline, and the difference between a granny knot and a reef knot, has the potential of being a good crew member.

There are a number of ways to acquire basic knowledge, along with the vocabulary of sailing. In addition to books, there are videos available that show as well as explain the fundamental principles of sailing a boat. It is recommended, however, that the beginner take a course at a sailing school. They are designed to give you on board 'hands on' experience. Sailing schools can be found at most harbours where large numbers of yachts are moored, and are advertised in any of the sailing magazines.

Apart from sailing, you may already possess some of the skills desired for crewing on a cruising yacht. Most can be acquired by enrolling in night courses in a community adult education programme. If no such programme is available in your area, some of the skills can be learnt through correspondence courses. Those that will be discussed fall into two categories. One has to do with the well-being of the crew, the other concerns the proper running and maintenance of the yacht, and although two categories have been drawn up for the purposes of discussion, the skills in each category are necessarily reliant on those in the other category.

Although some of these skills may not be as important as others, they will all add to the smooth running of a yacht, making the voyage more trouble-free and enjoyable. In fact the importance of any of these skills will vary according to the type of yacht and skipper concerned. If the skipper is a medical doctor in a boat with no engine, then obviously some skills will be of more interest to him than to the skipper with all the latest gadgetry and a family to take care of.

Health and Morale	*Yacht Maintenance*
Cooking	Diesel mechanics
Medical	Inventive engineering
Musical	Sewing
Languages	Navigation
Teaching/nanny	Radio, electronics and electricity
	Computer literacy
	Swimming and diving

Cooking

At the top of the list of desired skills is cooking. Often, the duties of cooking are rotated among the crew. The morale and well-being of the crew depends upon wholesome and tasty meals, and occasional 'treats' in the form of a cake or something similar. What can be prepared will depend on the type of cooking facilities, as well as storage or refrigeration facilities on board. Consequently you should organize yourself and prepare the sandwiches etc for the night watch and stow them safely and conveniently for the crew to eat when required, after dealing with the main meal in the daytime.

To cook on a yacht requires a person with a high degree of creativity, agility and organizational abilities. What is prepared for a meal often depends on the weather, as the motion of the boat will determine what can be cooked. Eating times are planned for the greatest convenience of the watch schedule. The preparation and eating of the main meal should be done in daylight hours to conserve battery power and to avoid problems with night navigation.

The cooks will also be responsible for conferring with the skipper on the purchase of food, depending on the local availability of food items, storage facilities, the number of people on board and the duration of the voyage. At each port a new inventory and a list of requirements will be needed. Once you are on a sea voyage you can't go to the shops for something you have forgotten or run out of, so this is an important part of passage planning.

So that you will be aware of the problems from the start read some of the cookery books that have been written by cruising people. They are worth reading to familiarize yourself with the special requirements of catering on a cruising yacht. Most boat owners have learnt from experience what types of food are best to buy and how they can best be stored and preserved with the facilities they have, and you will learn from them how they prefer to do things.

For example, some people like to grease eggs, some rely on systematically turning them, others can refrigerate them. Products like flour, sugar and tea which are not in a container for daily use must be kept dry. As this is a problem on a yacht these items have to be carefully packaged in addition to the packaging in which you buy them. Sometimes tinned food has to be stowed in the bilges or in lockers that will get wet, in which case each tin has to be varnished. Fresh vegetables have their own storage problems; most keep best in light airy conditions – hanging nets are ideal. However, this is not always possible and alternative areas have to be used such as the anchor chain locker.

Here are some simple guidelines to keep in mind. Of the raw meats you may decide to carry, fish will go bad first, then chicken and pork. Beef keeps longest and even improves with age. All meat keeps longer cooked. Of vegetables, salad ingredients go off first, then beans, cauliflower and carrots. Potatoes and onions can last a long time but they need to be turned and sorted regularly as one bad one can quickly affect the others. Cabbage lasts well, up to a month, and squashes last longest.

Of course, a voyage of two to four weeks will not create the same problems as a voyage of two to four months, and this should also be taken into consideration.

The acquisition of this kind of knowledge takes practice and experience. You will gain it as you go along, and yachties are always swapping useful tips with each other to overcome provisioning problems.

Medical

Because of the need for self-sufficiency on a cruising yacht, the medical supplies required will be much more extensive than a first aid kit can provide. They will include antibiotics and pain killers requiring a doctor's prescription for purchase. The need therefore exists for knowledge and skills in their use.

Doctors and nurses who choose to go cruising are much in demand, not only by fellow yachties but by people living in remote areas who have very little in the way of medical facilities. Anybody crewing who has medical skills is soon known on the grapevine of other yachts cruising in the same waters.

Musical

Musical instruments like guitars, flutes and harmonicas have a wonderful way of making people happy and lifting morale, whether for entertainment at sea or at an anchorage, where people like to get together to entertain each other. Musicians from different yachts often find themselves playing together, accompanied by others who like to sing.

Playing an instrument is a particular skill which not only enhances life at sea and is very welcome in remote anchorages with other yachties, but is also very popular with local inhabitants. To have the opportunity to give pleasure and have a good rapport with your hosts makes life enjoyable for everyone. These exchanges between cultures are part of the fun of cruising.

Languages

The major language used at sea is English, technically and socially, so a non-English-speaking person will find themselves at a disadvantage. The other languages widely used are French and Spanish. In addition to English, to be able to communicate in French and/or Spanish is of great help for translating to skipper and crew, dealing with port officials and papers, finding your way around on shore quickly, purchasing for the boat, and meeting local inhabitants and enjoying their country.

Teaching/nanny

More and more people cruise as a family, which means their children grow up outside of conventional educational institutions. The parent most qualified/suited thus has to take the responsibility for educating their offspring, usually with the aid of government-designed correspondence courses. For a crew member to be able to teach general subjects and take charge of the children for study hours, can be a valuable asset to cruising parents. There may well be times when there are several cruising families in a harbour at the same time, who would appreciate the skills of a teacher.

Children do very well cruising. The world is their classroom and they are usually more mature and responsible than their counterparts on shore. However, they can have problems with keeping abreast of the academic school curriculum without the advantage of a classroom environment.

Diesel mechanics

People with a diesel engine in their yachts will discuss their problems with it endlessly, so to have knowledge of diesel engineering is another of those most desirable skills. Mechanics need a good understanding and instinct under any circumstances, but at sea you need to be psychic! You need to be able to carry out good workable makeshift repairs and be prepared for contortions to squeeze into spaces of inhuman proportions. It is very different from working in a proper workshop.

Yachties tend to help each other out and help solve each other's problems in theory as well as practice, so you'll find yourself aiding others; your skills won't remain exclusive to the boat you are crewing on.

Inventive engineering

Some people are good 'fixers'. They can turn their hands to metalwork, woodwork, and can create ways of mending, repairing and manufacturing. If you do have this practical facility, you will be endlessly useful on board a cruising yacht and will be provided with many challenges. Remember, this is not a boat used for weekends or the odd holiday – it is in constant working use, the wear and tear is continuous, and the job of general maintenance is never ending. As a result, most yachts have an area set aside for storing 'workshop' materials and tools. It is an indispensable skill for this self-sufficient lifestyle.

Sewing

Everyone should be able to help sew and mend sails; it could be an essential safety factor. So, if you are good at sewing and have an understanding of materials, your skills will be valued for making and repairing sails, sailbags, lee cloths and upholstery. You will also find yourself in demand for repairing clothing, and even making clothes and other items for the boat. Many boats have sewing machines, but much of the heavy stuff has to be done by hand.

Courtesy flags often have to be made for the next foreign port. If these are needed, check that the right selection of coloured materials are aboard and that you have an accurate record of international flags that you can copy.

Navigation

Most skippers prefer to do their own navigation; after all, they are ultimately responsible for the boat's successful landfall. However, if you can navigate, the skipper will appreciate having you aboard as back up to help out at any time, and to take over if the skipper becomes incapacitated for any reason.

Everyone aboard should have some basic idea of navigation, to at least be able to enter useful comments in the log. Educating the rest of the crew in these matters could also be helpful.

Radio, electronics and electricity

If your skills lie in this area, they will come in very useful at sea. The proper operation and handling of a radio is important, as it is often the only means of communication with the outside world, and for obtaining weather reports. Ham radio operators are plentiful among yachties, who like to set up communication 'nets' with each other at sea. This serves as a self-help network as well as a means of social communication.

Electronic instruments for navigation, receiving weather

reports and radar, powered by energy from various sorts of equipment such as a generator, solar panels, windmills and water-spinners, are an important part of the yachtie's world. All these need to be understood and maintained.

The boat will probably have been wired up for electricity powered from the engine batteries and will rely on this system for navigational lights and conveniences. Electrical malfunctions are therefore always a potential problem on a yacht, and an understanding of electricity and the equipment is a definite asset.

Computer literacy

As a result of the improvements made for providing electric power mentioned previously, computers are being used more and more on yachts, particularly small, portable personal computers. Systems are available for interfacing all the ship's electronic instruments used for navigation: satellite navigation receiver, log, depthsounder, wind direction and speed indicator. Systems are capable of calculating the ship's position, course and leeway and of receiving weatherfax transmissions.

There are software programmes now for calculating ocean tides and currents, programmes presenting celestial navigation tables and almanacs and the List of Lights, as well as problem-solving programmes. There is lots of software available for the 'less experienced navigator' as well as the very technical in terms of navigation and computer literacy. Some programmes are designed specifically for racing. Electronic chart programmes are available that can be interfaced with an integrated instrument system, and some are capable of overlaying a radar image.

The UK Hydrographic Office has launched the Admiralty Raster Chart Service – 'ARCS' – distributed on CD-ROM which will be acceptable as an electronic version of paper charts for use with the Electronic Chart Systems (ECS) developed by equipment manufacturers. These are not officially recognized as being equivalent to paper charts for navigational purposes, although they are a suitable aid to navigation.

Many yacht owners rely on the traditional methods, carrying charts, books of all the mathematical tables required, a sextant, and other manual navigational aids, but as in any walk of life people like to take advantage of new developments as and when they can. Private yachts will inevitably become equipped with more sophisticated equipment benefiting from new technology as a matter of course. Be cautious of sailing with a skipper who has not retained the basic methods as a backup to electronic equipment and computerised systems as the sea environment is notoriously bad for electronic components and the source of electric power cannot always be guaranteed.

One needs to be able to understand the basic principles and navigational terms in order to understand the programmes, but being computer literate is a great advantage if these systems are to be used to their best potential.

Swimming and diving

Work has to be done on the boat's hull from time to time, and thus being a good swimmer and free diver is a great help to the skipper. If things are lost overboard at anchor, they are often retrievable by a good swimmer – and they may often be important items. Additionally, anchors and lines quite frequently become tangled up while under water and have to be freed. There are plenty of people who live at sea who are not efficient swimmers, so an ability in this area is often appreciated.

Some boats carry aqualungs and compressors for diving pleasure; these are also an advantage for dealing with an underwater problem. Sometimes boats will carry just an aqualung solely for use in emergencies. If you are a certified diver, this is a skill you can contribute. It may be that you have your own gear which you can arrange to take with you, to mutual advantage.

Photography

Since this skill does not really fit into either of the categories on p 32, and does not often serve a truly *useful* purpose on a private cruise, it is only mentioned here to suggest that a professional photographer is frequently required on cruises mounted as special projects or for expeditions mounted by universities and other bodies. However, it is advisable to be pretty familiar with life at sea to be able to concentrate properly on the job of photography.

Conclusion

It is interesting that some cruising yachts seem to go from one misadventure to another and other yachts proceed smoothly with no apparent problems at all. This difference is probably a consequence of the skipper's attention to details and to skill in preplanning the voyage. It could also be a reflection of the individual skills of those on board.

Practical advice

The foregoing advice about which particular skills could be desirable to a skipper looking for crew needs to be followed by a few tips on how to prepare yourself to best fulfil your skills, and what to take along.

Cooking

If you intend to claim cooking as a skill that you can contribute, don't go empty-handed. You will need inspiration, so have your favourite cookery book with you, or a compilation of your most useful recipes. A table of conversions for weights and measures between pounds and ounces, kilos and grams, and pints and litres, and in addition a table of these measures in terms of cups and spoons, will save headaches and dilemmas when your recipe's measurements don't match the equipment on board.

Can you bake bread? This is an essential at sea. Can you produce more than half a dozen ways of cooking fresh tuna fish? Be prepared!

Be prepared also to be called to help on deck at any time while cooking. Devise a procedure for the swift stowage of everything that could spill when left unattended, preferably wedging containers into the sink.

Medical

If the skipper is agreeable, you can ask to check what medicines he has and, if necessary, suggest any improvements in the supplies. Then, if you are called upon to assist, you will be sure of having the basic requirements instead of assuming the skipper will have everything you need.

Individuals are advised to be as self-sufficient as possible, and not to rely on the boat's medical kit. Obviously, you will have to take a proper supply of any personal medicines that you know you require. Go to your GP and tell him what you plan to do, and ask for at least one full course of a broad spectrum antibiotic tablet, a broad spectrum antibiotic powder and cream, a tube of antibiotic eye ointment, and also get basic instructions from him. Have a bottle of surgical spirit and a supply of cotton wool and dressings with you to take care of small wounds immediately, as they can quickly turn into tropical ulcers or festering sores. Make sure you have the right inoculations and malaria tablets. Lastly, it's not a bad idea to have a supply of multivitamin pills.

Consider taking a first aid course run by an organization like St John's Ambulance. Knowing proper procedures in the event of an accident could minimize the risk of serious consequences developing in the absence of professionals.

Musical

The sea is not a good environment for string instruments and they take up a good deal of space – probably your space – so work out a way your guitar can be properly stowed and take plenty of extra strings. Take sheet music too; *you* may know the piece but somebody else might like to play with you. Have words for the pieces that can be sung; people usually know the tune but often don't remember the words, and many a well-intentioned sing-along dies for lack of them.

Languages

Check out the main languages used in the areas you intend to visit and brush up on them, especially for technical terms such as diesel engines and parts, and boat parts with which you may not ordinarily be familiar. You may want to invest in a yachtsman's pocket dictionary that gives boat parts in a variety of languages.

Teaching

American, Canadian, Australian, New Zealand and British Departments of Education have correspondence courses available for children who cannot, under ordinary circumstances, attend school, and most yachtie parents avail themselves of these facilities. Check the syllabuses and the books used in the subjects you teach, so that you know what is required.

Diesel mechanics

Do some research on marinized diesel engines; Perkins, Ford and Volvo Penta are the most used. Check that the skipper has the proper manual for the engine and that no pages are missing. Talk to the skipper about the spare parts carried and the tools on board for the job. Take your own overalls; there won't be any others.

Sewing

If there is a sewing machine on board, familiarize yourself with it before you have to 'perform' on it. Sewing machines on boats only require zig-zag and straight stitch. Rusting at sea is a problem even with stainless steel, so keep the machine well oiled – oil it each time you use it as salt crystals will be in the fabrics stitched. Make sure it has the operator's manual and plenty of needles, including lots of heavyweight ones.

Books are available on the subject of sail maintenance and repair, so familiarize yourself with how sails are made and how to fix them. Check that there is a sail 'palm' and proper sailcloth thread and needles on board for the handwork, and a reference book. All needles, pins and scissors should be lubricated, or they will rust quickly at sea.

Crew should carry their own basic sewing kits to be able to take care of their personal mending requirements.

Navigation

If you hope to put your skills into action, have your own navigation pack. Consider taking a cheap sextant, your own navigational calculator, and any books and worksheets that *you* are used to. Check that there is an efficient time signal receiver on board, so that you can go efficiently into action instead of trying to take over someone else's practices.

Radio, electronics and electricity

Everybody aboard should be familiar with the correct procedure for using VHF radio telephones and GMDSS (Global Maritime Distress & Safety System) at sea for ordinary communications and emergencies. Most governments require operators to pass a test and obtain a certificate of competency; this may not be required of you, but it is as well to know the correct procedures.

The Royal Yachting Association or the Coast Guard can provide all the necessary information.

If electronics or electricity is your speciality, check that the right manuals and tools are available: soldering iron and solder, amp meter, volt meter, extra wiring, electrical tape, etc.

Computer literacy

If you have computer or programming skills and would like to know more about what is on the market for yacht navigation purposes you can get information from: Tim Thornton at Maritime Computing International Ltd, Hamble Court, Hamble Lane, Hamble, Southampton SO31 4QJ. Tel: 02380 458047, Fax: 02380 458057, Email: sales@marinecomputing.com, Website: www.marinecomputing.com. Should you have your own PC or laptop and you are joining a skipper who is computer orientated you could offer to take it along to complement the existing instrumentation, or as a backup to the ship's computer providing you transfer the existing programme in advance.

Photography

If photography is your hobby, you will probably already have the necessary knowledge and equipment to take with you for a record of your voyage. Extra items to consider taking are waterproof carrying pouches and special filters and lens hoods for protection from the reflection of tropic sun on water.

Slide processing is often not available in remote areas. A good way to overcome the problem of processing slide film, without keeping it too long in a humid environment, is to take along special 'mail order' film processing envelopes. Even so, it may sometimes be a month before you can send them off, so take silica for storing both exposed and unexposed film.

Personal gear

The skipper will assume that as a competent crew member you will have organized your personal requirements properly. Don't pack a suitcase; take a strong nylon holdall that is thoroughly collapsible and stowable. Travel as light as you possibly can – there is very little space on a yacht, and crew seem to be expected to have no baggage to speak of anyway. One smart set of clothes is enough. In some countries, shorts are not acceptable in public places, banks, restaurants, bars, official offices and places of interest. Sometimes women are required to wear discreet skirts and keep their arms covered. A track suit is handy, but mostly you'll use T-shirts and shorts. (Incidentally, old T-shirts make popular gifts to islanders.) Cloth sun hats or visors are essential for protection from the glare. Have a pair of proper deck shoes with you, and of course some rubber sandals to protect the soles of your feet in public showers.

Stow your clothes in plastic bags to keep them dry. Make sure your documents and money are in a waterproof holder, which is especially useful for going ashore by dinghy when they are liable to get wet in transit. Keep a separate record of passport, visas, tickets, charge cards and traveller's cheque numbers. If you wear glasses or contact lenses, have two pairs with you, and a copy of your prescription. Wear your glasses and sunglasses with an elastic strap to prevent them from being whipped overboard.

You will need a sleeping bag or lightweight bedding (sometimes just a sheet will do) and your own towel. Ordinary soap does not lather in sea water; use your shampoo as body soap as well. A sunblock is essential for lips and nose.

Take your own foul weather gear and harness. Boats should be equipped with enough harnesses, but take your own and be sure of it; the same applies to a good lifejacket. There are brands that incorporate harnesses and lightweight lifevests.

Have with you a small waterproof torch, spare bulbs and batteries; some skippers will not allow lights after dark. In any case, with a torch you are less likely to disturb other people when you are preparing to go on and off watch. Remember to take your personal stereo, medical requirements, and sewing kit.

Safety

There are important safety rules which are part of the science of sailing and learned accordingly. They are the usual things that are taught like, keeping your head out of the way of the boom, keeping your fingers out of the line you are winching, wearing a safety harness, clipping on at the right places, using the bosun's chair properly, and following the principle of 'one hand for you, one for the boat'. There are other important safety rules governing your movements in relation to other vessels, both on the open sea and in coastal channels, similar to the highway code. There is also a range of safety factors that need to be considered as part of life at sea which are not always so obvious to everyone. Like, don't jump off the boat when it is under way! It has been known for a crew member on watch to jump off the yacht to rescue a line, a cushion or some other object they were responsible for when the vessel was going three knots or less, thinking that it was going so slowly that they would be good enough swimmers to catch up with the boat, or they would be able to grab at a part of the boat in passing to hold on. It doesn't work; it creates a high risk situation known as 'man overboard' which may be a matter of life and death. Similarly males on deck alone urinating over the side have been known to lose concentration letting go of the rigging and a sudden lurch has put them into the same predicament. Beware too of a similar possibility when hauling a bucket of sea water on to the deck. Don't allow the bucket to drag and don't let go of the boat or else the bucket could haul you into the sea. Small children can get over excited when they see friends or parents coming alongside in the dinghy and literally walk over the side into the water, forgetting they are not in a house where they can run out to greet someone. When it is feasible to swim, make sure you can get back on board. Check that a ladder is out or the dinghy is alongside to provide access to the yacht.

Sometimes the main gangway on a yacht has a hatch cover of clear Perspex material. More people have suffered from a severe knock on the head and neck injuries by coming up the gangway with momentum, thinking it was open, than have been hit on the head by a boom. Take notice of what jobs the skipper has on the agenda, maybe lifelines and stanchions that you automatically rely on are removed to be worked on. Or you could come confidently down the gangway and land in the bilges risking an injury because the cabin sole has been taken up for some project. If your bunk is equipped with a lee board or lee cloth use it when you sleep, the crew on watch may have to tack and you could be tossed out of your bed with most unfortunate side effects.

In the galley specific operational rules apply when using the cooker or stove in the same way as with the vessel's pumps. There are hazards attached to using either bottled gas or kerosene which are the two types of fuel generally used on yachts. In both cases you should get instructions from the skipper on the methods and precautions used for priming, lighting, using and switching off safely to avoid the dangerous results of leakages. The cooker could qualify as one of the most dangerous pieces of equipment on board, and when improperly, or too casually, used has the potential of setting fire to, or blowing up, the yacht, and this has been the cause of the loss of far too many yachts.

The cooker, or stove, in the galley should be recessed into a space where it can be gimballed, allowing it always to swing to a horizontal plane with the motion of the boat when in use. This reduces the likelihood of hot pots, pans and their contents flying off the surface. Many cookers have pot clamps too. There should be a strong stainless steel bar called a 'crash-bar' firmly inserted across the front of the stove recess, so called because should the cook lose their balance they will crash into the bar rather than into the lighted stove. Some people recommend that when cooking in the galley you should be fully protected by wearing your foul weather suit. However, under most circumstances a plastisized apron should protect you adequately from most spills and splashes, but some protection should be worn. Burns occur most frequently in the galley and they should be treated immediately, so there should be a good burn ointment handy in the galley drawer. Most well-found yachts will have fire extinguishers in several locations on board including the engine compartment, and there should be one in the galley as well as a fire blanket.

When you are on watch you must be alert. You may be responsible not only for steering the yacht, but for everything that is happening on and around it. You must be aware, looking at the sea, the sails, the equipment in front of you and behind you all the time. The rest of the people on board are relying on you to do a good job watching out for sunken logs, lost containers from commercial vessels, fishing nets, passing ships, sleeping whales, sudden squalls and pirates.

During the day it is easy to be distracted by other people's activities and conversations, or events like catching a fish. At night when there is little companionship it is easy to day dream, become mesmerised by the rhythmic motion of the boat and the waves, or distracted by phospherescent lights in the water. You can simply fall asleep, losing control of the ship's course or maybe accidentally gybing the boat. When you are on watch the safety of the yacht and everyone on board is in your hands and you must prepare for watches properly, anticipating your personal needs, dressing properly against the sun or the cold, and resting as best you can when off duty so that you can be as responsible as possible on watch.

In times of stress or storms it is best for everyone to try to maintain the watch schedule so that the whole crew does not get too exhausted, creating a situation where no one can function well. Never worry about waking or calling the skipper if a situation is developing which you feel is out of your control, whether it is for assistance to tie down a loose line, readjust the sails, for a change in the weather, or for the proximity of another vessel. It is best not to take unilateral decisions without informing the skipper as they need to know everything that is happening in case it affects the navigation of the yacht or some other important aspect.

Safety is an important part of sailing and it has been found from experience that rules have to be followed, and that there are these other types of situations – almost comical – which can also turn into serious safety hazards.

There is another subject that should be mentioned here and that is many skippers sailing outside European waters will carry firearms for the protection of the yacht and crew. There is a certain amount of controversy as to whether the carrying of firearms encourages violent situations rather than preventing them, nevertheless firearms on board are a fact of life on most boats sailing in remote areas and those places that have a reputation for piracy.

Living on board

To live on board requires a certain amount of specialized knowledge about yachts and how they function both domestically, and as ocean-going vessels. As such, humans must learn to operate comfortably in them.

Some of these points have already been covered under other headings but they are gathered together here under one heading in order to present a more complete domestic picture.

We have talked about respect for the boat and its equipment. It's up to the skipper to show you how he or she would like things handled, but it's also up to you to find out and ask about things rather than make presumptions and use equipment incorrectly, possibly causing damage – you would be surprised just how easy it is to do this.

Every item on board has been stowed where it is for some reason, for example for safety, protection, convenience, or comfort. The skipper knows where everything is kept and expects everything always to be in its place. Never use a tool, utensil, book, torch or any equipment without returning it to the place in which you found it – and *as* you found it. This is important as some items sit one way better than another and can get jammed if they are not stowed at the right angle, or they may rattle and bang with the yacht's motion.

Equipment like the yacht's tender has to be used in a planned and considerate way. The dinghy is the yacht's lifeline to the shore in many harbours, and is used for taking care of business, provisioning, pleasure outings, socializing and visiting other yachts. Rather like the family car, it will be hard to make it suit everybody's needs and requirements all the time, and certain things will necessarily take priority. For example, you can't borrow the tender for half an hour and not bother to return for two or three hours because during that time other people will need it. It is a very important part of the yacht's equipment, and while you are using it you are responsible for its safekeeping. You will be expected to take proper precautions against its theft, and to avoid its loss by tying it up carefully, as well as preventing unnecessary wear and tear or damage. A yacht without a tender is in a very inconvenient situation indeed, and, unlike the family car, there are often no alternatives like taxis, buses and trains to cross a stretch of water between the yacht and land.

We have touched on the proper use of VHF and radio, the music system, conservation of the ship's battery power and water supply. And we have considered the proper provisioning and planning of food, which should be used sensibly and imaginatively. People who eat up special provisions and treats selfishly are soon invited to leave.

We've referred to the 24-hour day and the work involved.

You should bear in mind that there *is* work to do, maybe not of the sort you're used to, but tasks that must be completed, pleasant or not. One of the problems about giving up a conventional lifestyle to do something different like going on a sailing adventure, is that some people find it difficult to come to terms with the fact that work still has to be done and instructions still have to be carried out. You may find yourself doing harder jobs, ones that take longer, and jobs of a nature you would never dream of undertaking in any other circumstances, as well as complying with orders in a way you have never been used to before. There are times at sea when you will almost certainly be expected to perform the seemingly impossible!

While accommodating and coping with these challenges, you will see how important all the socio-cultural issues can become in a life afloat. Also important is respect for other people's space and keeping to your own. It is essential for your own sake and for those in close proximity to you to keep your own gear stowed properly, to keep yourself clean and healthy, and to remember the yachties' code of etiquette. People coping with the pressures of new challenges in the confined quarters of a boat cannot afford to overlook any of these aspects.

The yacht itself doesn't make life on board easy either. Since yachts are designed for optimum efficiency in moving through water and not necessarily for human comfort (although a lot has been achieved in modern design to alleviate this problem), it means that living arrangements and living spaces are awkward compared with land-based dwellings, so you have to develop a particular agility that is peculiar to life afloat.

You have to learn where strong handholds are and respond to them automatically so that you don't grab something fragile when there is an unexpected lurch. Learn how to brace yourself when performing various tasks so that you don't fall and break your arm or the equipment you may be handling. You must become aware of head space when coming through hatches, keeping clear of booms and boom-braces, and be able to move smoothly through the rigging. You have to adapt to walking on a deck that is continually coming up to meet your feet instead of staying still while you put your feet down. It's well known that sailors have a curious walk when on land and it's quite true that after a period of time at sea, walking on terra firma is an odd sensation. People tend to overlook the problems associated with the motion of a small vessel at sea as you do have to acquire the art of compensating for the yacht's motion continually, even when sleeping – acquiring a few bruises while you do so. Yachties often joke that the only comfortable places on a boat at sea are being flat on your back in your bunk or holding on to the helm.

Related to this is the reason why cooking requires such a high degree of creativity, agility and organizational ability. You can never leave pots and pans or plates of food and drinks unattended. The same applies to tools; nothing remains in place for long when in use. Everything has to be stowed properly.

Doors and lockers on yachts cannot just be opened and closed; they are all equipped with special latches so that they don't fly open at sea. These safety latches must always be used properly so that doors don't bang and lockers don't spill their contents. If it is possible to open them, portholes and hatches must be monitored carefully. It is no good forgetting you opened a porthole or hatch when the skipper decides to tack, or the weather gets bad. The consequences will be large quantities of sea water or rain in the cabin, which is always to be avoided.

Moisture below decks creates dampness, mildew, odours and general discomfort that is almost impossible to get rid of. Foul weather gear must be taken off with care and hung in the most appropriate place, not thrown on the couch. Any furnishings or bedding that get wet will not dry easily in the sea environment, and it probably won't be possible to dry things properly until you get to port, which could be weeks later. Even if you are careful, you will generally have to bring everything out for an airing whenever possible. For the first few days in a port, most boats are festooned with bedding, clothing and couch cushions.

The other more important aspect of keeping the boat dry and afloat is the hull and its through-hull fittings and pumps, an aspect that people living in houses never have to consider.

The yacht's hull has to be watertight, and ideally there should be no holes where water can enter to fill the hull and potentially sink the boat. However, nothing in life is ideal, so we have to live with the problem of holes in the hull – through-hull fittings to accommodate the engine's cooling water intake and output, the galley sink, the heads, and general leakage and drainage for rainwater and waves. To control this situation, every hole in the hull is fitted with a seacock which can seal the hull when necessary or in an emergency. They are operated by levers inside the boat on the hoses and drains they are specifically designed to control. Hence, many of the lockers or cupboards you open will have a large metal seacock control lever in them. This tends to limit the use of certain spaces, since easy, quick access to these levers is required at all times. A skipper diving into a cupboard to grab a seacock lever, only to find it buried under a pile of belongings, will throw the latter out unceremoniously. Never turn any seacock controls without knowing whether you are opening or closing them; you might sink the boat! If you do turn any seacocks you must tell your skipper.

The next set of controls are the boat's pumps. They play an important part in keeping the yacht afloat. There are various types for various jobs. The engine has pumps for fuel and water and it is usually set in its own bilge because of the oily nature of the engine and the maintenance jobs that have to be performed; this area will have its own bilge pump. There are usually other pumps placed strategically in the boat's bilges for pumping out water that collects through condensation and general seepage. Sometimes shower water from the heads drains into the bilge and has to be pumped clear.

Some pumps are electric, some automatic, some manual, but all have to be kept clean and free for efficient operation. These pumps are used both in daily living and in an emergency. One of the problems is that these pumps are mostly situated under the cabin sole. This means that any dirt or debris that falls on the floor may work its way into the bilge and clog the pump. So it is important to keep the floor cleared and clean. The main offenders are small metal objects that will rust in the bilge and will jam the pump mechanism; small nails, pins, paperclips, staples, hairgrips, toothpicks and bits of plastic are the main culprits. Thread-ends off clothes or from sewing jobs and bits of string can wrap around the pump mechanism and jam it; so can human hair, so you have to keep control of loose hairs when brushing and combing.

Then we come to the heads. The toilet on a yacht cannot be a flush toilet like those in a house, or on a liner or ferry. It also has to be operated by pump. Sea water is pumped into the toilet bowl before use and shut off. After the toilet has been used it has to be pumped clear, flushed through, then pumped dry and shut off. This is the most problematic of all the ship's pumps and causes endless grief if not used properly. It is often the first area over which skipper and crew relationships collapse – so be warned. Remember, it is essential to shut off the pump in preparation for using the toilet and on completion, or else the ocean could seize the opportunity to flow into the bowl! Remember too that the toilet must be flushed through properly because the piping is very convoluted due to the confined space and in an effort to reduce the risk of overflow. Much careful pumping is therefore necessary to clear the hoses or else blockages will occur. A blockage means somebody has to dismantle the hoses and pump to clear them – need we say more!

On this subject it is essential to point out that absolutely nothing except human waste can be accommodated by a yacht's heads. An excess of toilet paper, or any cotton wool, tampons, cigarette ends, etc cannot be allowed to go through the pump system. There are usually written instructions on all heads, because all have small operational variations. Ask the skipper to give you a proper demonstration, and keep on asking for demonstrations until you get it absolutely right; they won't mind. If you are visiting another yacht and you are not certain of the correct operation of the heads, do ask the skipper.

There are pumps too for bringing water up from the water tanks to the galley and sometimes to basins in the heads. They can be hand or foot operated or electrically operated. Malfunctioning pumps of this kind cannot sink the boat, but equal care has to be taken with them or you will not be able to draw from the ship's water supply.

Lastly, there will be drains on deck in the cockpit to allow rain water and waves to drain out through the hull. A blockage in one of these could allow the cockpit to fill like a bathtub and flood the boat, so these drains have to be kept clean and clear. The same applies to the scuppers and drains around the decks, or the decks won't clear quickly enough.

Much of what has been said here may sound tedious and make life on board seem very inconvenient. To some extent it is, but these are the things that you will have to get used to if you are considering the cruising lifestyle. However, one becomes accustomed to these differences and they soon become natural and automatic; but by anticipating these aspects, you will save yourself and the skipper many potential problems.

Living arrangements at sea and in port

There are two different lifestyles on a cruising yacht, depending on whether the boat is at sea or in port.

It has already been mentioned that at sea the need to keep the yacht moving forward on the desired course as fast, as safely and as comfortably as possible under varying weather conditions is the reason for a 24-hour day, and the necessity to eat and sleep at abnormal times.

The yacht's motion, according to the weather and point of sailing, is also a strong influence on routines at sea. For example, the least desirable part of the boat to sleep in is the bow, where there is the most motion. The centre of the boat, amidships, is the most stable part, which is why most galleys are situated here. If there is an aft cabin, it is usually the next most stable area. In any of these areas, the lower you are relative to the centre of gravity, ie the floor, the more stable you will find it. The higher the bunk, the more likelihood of being tossed out of it in heavy weather if there is no lee cloth or lee board.

Not every voyage will experience heavy weather, of course, but in any event it is as well to be flexible about sleeping and eating areas while at sea in order to be as comfortable as possible under the prevailing circumstances. So to sleep on the floor or in the main living area of the boat rather than in your allotted cabin or bunk, or to wedge yourself into a corner holding on to your plate, is a sensible approach at these times.

Everything has to have its place and be properly stowed on a boat at sea. This applies to the yacht's equipment as well as your own belongings. You can't afford to leave anything out of place, since equipment will quickly be damaged, and personal gear will make the boat disorderly – and a disorderly boat can quickly become a dangerous environment.

While in port, the forward cabin in the bow is by contrast often the most desirable place for sleeping. Swinging at anchor you will have good ventilation through the forward hatch, which can't always be open at sea, providing a pleasant, private place. Sleeping in the cockpit is cool and spacious and can also be very comfortable in port in the tropics, providing there is some sort of awning for protection against rain.

Although the same sort of watch routine is not necessary for manning the boat in port, participation in the maintenance and preparation of the boat will always be required.

When in port, there is the opportunity to prepare and eat meals in a more relaxed manner. In cooler climates it is nice to be in a cosy, warm atmosphere around the saloon table to eat, and maybe to entertain fellow yachties. In the tropics, people will prefer to eat and relax in the cockpit, rigging up outside lighting and a table to take advantage of the warm evenings outside.

The ability to be flexible and change smoothly from the routine of life at sea to life in port will be reflected in the degree of comfort and pleasure a person can experience.

Seasickness

You can presume that to a greater or lesser degree you are likely to suffer from seasickness for some of the time at sea – and, in some unfortunate cases, all of the time.

Most people are either sick or feel queasy, or are lethargic and generally uncomfortable from the motion of the yacht for the first three days. After this, the body learns to adjust to the motion of the boat and most people overcome the problem.

The last thing a skipper needs is a seasick crew, and the last thing the crew needs is to be seasick; so before you set sail, at least four hours beforehand, take precautions so that whatever preventative you choose to use is already working in your system so that you can be useful and active once under way.

The first three days or so will be a little difficult and strange while people get used to each other, the boat and the duties on board, so you should try to avoid feeling ill at this time. Spend as much time as you can on deck. You are less likely to suffer from seasickness if you are out in the fresh air and can see a horizon, which gives your body a point of reference for balance. Remember to breathe deeply if you start feeling queasy. Try to eat simple, nutritious, non-greasy and non-spicy foods; don't skip meals and have an empty stomach, and don't drink alcohol. Above all, don't get drunk the night before you leave and acquire a hangover – have that party a couple of days before you leave.

Preparing food in the galley is probably the job most conducive to bringing on seasickness – below decks in a small confined space, probably with little air circulating. In addition, there will be the heat from the stove and the smells and textures of the food you are preparing. Similar conditions apply when working on the engine. Make a point of coming out on deck at regular intervals to look around and breathe fresh air deeply.

Prepare the first main meal of a voyage before departure, and make it something that simply needs to be reheated – like a casserole or a stew. Have sandwiches made up for a lighter meal and stowed in a plastic box. This will be a great advantage. Before you leave shore, plan simple easy meals for the next few days, possibly cooking meat in advance so that it can be eaten cold.

The first three days of any voyage, even when you have been sailing for a while and have then stopped over somewhere for a week or more, are the most likely days for seasickness; but you may also have a problem if you run into a storm or a situation that gives an unusual or different motion, so act promptly with your remedy on these occasions too. Some people are more affected than others, and you will have to learn what your tolerance is. Conditions at sea are ever-changing and are rarely the same for long periods, so seasickness caused by the boat's motion is only a temporary condition and will eventually pass. It should be mentioned that the effectiveness of any oral medication is seriously reduced as a result of continual vomiting and those people reliant on important medication should seek medical advice on their condition in relation to seasickness.

Although this has already been mentioned earlier in the book it should be repeated here, even though the medical profession might not acknowledge seasickness as a cause of pregnancy, that women taking oral contraception should keep this in mind as excessive or continual vomiting can reduce the effect of the Pill enough to allow pregnancy to occur.

Remedies

There are various remedies, and it is best to try different ones to see which suits you best. One of the most effective is scopo-

FEDERICO GARCIA LORCA'S

BLOOD WEDDING

May 19, 20, 21, 26, 27, 28 @ 7:30
May 22 and 28 @ 2:00

HEARTWOOD REGIONAL THEATER COMPANY

Heartwood Regional Theater Company
P.O. Box 1115
Damariscotta, ME 04543

BLOOD WEDDING

TRANSLATED BY LILLIAN GROAG

WITH JUANITO PASCUAL - FLAMENCO GUITAR

DIXIE WEISMAN - CHOREOGRAPHER
GRIFF BRALEY - ARTISTIC DIRECTOR

WISCASSET HIGH SCHOOL, WISCASSET, ME
TICKETS: 563-1373 OR heartwoodrtc@gwi.net
WWW.HEARTWOODTHEATER.ORG

SPONSORED BY DEAD RIVER COMPANY

PRODUCED WITH SPECIAL PERMISSION OF
DRAMATISTS PLAY SERVICE, INC.

lamine, a substance which can be absorbed through the skin behind the ear on a time-release system. Brand names for this are Transdermscop in the USA and Scoperderm in the UK and it is only available on prescription. There are some countries where it is available without prescription.

A highly recommended oral remedy which helps to balance the inner ear and needs no prescription is called Stugeron. It is available in most countries. Although these remedies are generally considered to be the most effective, they don't work for everyone and there are many other products on the market. Remember that your favourite remedy may not always be available, so don't forget to take a good supply with you.

Another anti-nausea measure, in the form of elasticated fabric wristbands (one to be worn on each wrist), depends on pressure being applied to the inside of the wrist, working along similar principles to techniques of acupressure. These wrist bands are suitable for adults and children, need no prescription, and are available in most European countries.

Seasickness in its worst form can be a very serious and debilitating problem if you are susceptible. Even if you are not so badly affected, be well prepared for it mentally by understanding that you may not feel a hundred percent, that it is a temporary condition, take immediate steps to relieve the situation, and be prepared for it practically by having medication with you, and handy.

Financial and Administrative Preparation

Financial responsibilities to skipper and authorities

There are two areas of financial responsibility when you crew on a yacht: to the skipper, and to the authorities of countries visited.

It must be understood that a skipper of a yacht entering a foreign country is responsible for their crew; this is mainly a financial matter. The skipper's credibility is established by the proof of ownership, or proof of employment as skipper of the yacht that they arrived on, which also guarantees their exit.

A crew member must establish his or her own financial credibility. It is therefore necessary to travel with enough funds to be able to fulfil the requirements of the country's immigration authorities. If you are to leave the yacht in a foreign port, either as arranged or because of a change of plan, you cannot be signed off the yacht unless you have a return ticket to your country of origin, or enough money to cover the cost of a ticket and to support yourself until departure. As a result of these requirements, you can expect the skipper to ask you for your airline ticket, or to deposit cash funds/traveller's cheques with them in the order of £500 or US$800 as a safeguard. It may be that you transfer to another yacht, in which case the skipper of that yacht will guarantee your departure. If you do transfer from one yacht to another, be sure to get signed off the boat on which you arrived and signed on to the new yacht *by the authorities*.

If you are flying into a foreign port to meet a yacht, you must have a letter from the skipper of the yacht indicating to the authorities that you are to be signed on as crew and will leave the country by yacht. Otherwise, you may be asked to place a money bond with the immigration department to cover the cost of a return flight. This money bond will be refunded when you have signed on as crew at the port of your departure, and have informed the authorities of the departure date.

Some countries, such as French Polynesia in the South Pacific (which includes the Marquesas Islands, Tuamotu Archipelago, and the Society Islands to which Tahiti and Bora Bora belong), require that each person visiting on a yacht, including the skipper, post a cash bond which is equal to the amount of their airfare home. This is kept by the authorities until the yacht's day of departure. Currently the bond is in the order of £1000 or US$1500 per person, even though the visa requirements for members of the European Union are the same as if you were visiting France. Regulations should be checked in advance with the consulate in the country prior to entry. Although this is a fact of life, there is no 'official' knowledge of it outside of this area.

Although there may not be the same cash bond problems for Europeans sailing in European waters, it could easily become a problem for North American and Commonwealth crew. However, for long distance voyages and journeys to remoter places, skippers will require this return ticket/cash bond to be available before signing you on as crew, and may require to have it deposited with them before sailing to cover their responsibility for you with the authorities.

More of a financial problem to the skipper rather than the crew are the local regulations for yacht equipment. International boats should not be affected as they are governed by the rules of their flag state, but they have been affected, and the International Maritime Organisation (IMO) has yet to introduce a standard worldwide. This matter has been brought to the attention of the yachting world by the legal battle ensuing from New Zealand safety laws. If the yacht's equipment does not comply with regulations on departure, you could be indirectly compromised, and subjected to inconveniences, delays and inevitably expenses. At the time of writing, yachts carrying less than twelve passengers should not be affected.

Financial arrangements with skipper and yacht

There are three types of sailing yacht that you may choose to travel on as crew: charter, cruising, or delivery. The cost of crewing will depend on the financial arrangements as prescribed by the skipper/owner and will be met in one of four ways:

A daily set fee
On a shared basis
No charge at all
Employment as paid crew

Charter fees

To charge a crew member on a daily basis, and make a profit, a yacht skipper should have a charter licence from the country in whose waters the yacht is sailing. It is illegal in most countries to operate a charter service and charge crew for a profit without a special charter licence.

Crewing on a charter yacht will require no particular skills on your part, although you will normally be expected to help in sailing the boat. This will be the most expensive way of experiencing the yachtie lifestyle. You can expect to pay, depending on the location, time of year and size of yacht, anywhere from £300 (US$450) to £1000+ (US$1500+) per day to cruise, at the time of writing.

The most popular areas for charter yachts are the Caribbean from November to May, and the Mediterranean from May to October; also, in the South Pacific all the year round. There are a few yachts that operate around-the-world trips; a prospective crew member can usually arrange to join them at various places and times around the world. If you are going aboard a charter yacht for the first time in a foreign port, financial arrangements will have to be made prior to leaving and the money paid to the charter boat's agent in the country of registration.

Shared expenses

To crew on a cruising yacht on a shared basis is probably to experience the most pleasure, along with a feeling of satisfaction in accomplishment – at probably the lowest cost with the largest amount of involvement. Surprisingly enough, you will also be maintaining more individual independence, for to be paying more than actual cost (or, at the opposite end, being paid to crew) will mean less individual freedom. With careful planning and proper preparation, it is possible to experience the cruising lifestyle as a crew member (excluding connecting travel costs), at less cost, on a daily basis, than staying at home. This is achieved by sharing expenses, duties and responsibilities, and perhaps by sailing to places where your money has more purchasing power.

What are the expenses shared by crew? This must be established by the prospective crew member with the skipper before coming aboard. The normal shared expenses aboard a cruising yacht are: food, fuel (diesel, petrol, stove), port and mooring fees. Upkeep of the yacht is usually covered by the crew's labour on a daily basis, but this must be established with the skipper beforehand and the items to be shared understood.

Alcoholic or soft drinks can be paid for from the yacht's food kitty, or as an extra, depending on the skipper. If it is part of the yacht's normal expense, then everybody aboard will agree on the daily consumption. It is generally accepted that all expenses incurred ashore and off the boat – such as eating out, recreation and travel – are extras paid for by the individual.

What will it cost on a shared-expense basis on a cruising yacht? As we have said, crewing is not simply a travel ticket. The actual cost will depend on the type of skipper, type of yacht, the degree of your participation and experience. With these variables to take into account, it is almost impossible to give a guideline as to costs.

The combinations of type of skipper, type of boat, type of accommodation and equipment, standard of living, are endless. For instance, if the boat is small and simple and the basic cost of cruising for the skipper is low, your contribution is going to be at the minimum end of the scale. If the boat is large but basic, and the skipper's need is for a large crew to handle the yacht, this will also mean your contribution will be low. Because of the large number of people involved, the cost of harbour fees and maintenance costs will be spread, accommodation is basic, and it is in the skipper's interest to make it financially attractive to the people they rely on to help sail the yacht.

A yacht of medium size with a few people on board, well equipped with refrigeration, heads with showers and comfortable accommodation and privacy in berths, along with labour-saving equipment and electronics, will reflect a different standard of living, affecting the type of food you are able to carry and also the higher costs of maintenance and upkeep for the skipper. Your share in a situation like this will obviously be higher. Also, the skipper will be less reliant on crew to help them as the equipment makes handling the boat easier.

Some people are happy with communal living and eating plenty of rice and beans. Other sailors like to cruise on a yacht that affords plenty of comforts and to get as close as they can to gourmet eating. Some boats are built with materials like steel and ferrocement, which makes hulls and decks less expensive to take care of than boats built of fibreglass and special woods. All these factors will be reflected in the cost of cruising.

Your contribution towards expenses will vary according to what it includes; sometimes it will be all the costs, sometimes just food and drink. If a skipper has put all their money into purchasing a yacht and requires crew to finance the provisioning and cruising of the vessel, your contribution may be higher than that with a skipper who already has a properly prepared yacht and still has funds for cruising.

Most skippers are fair about how they estimate the cruising costs for their own particular situation and the value of crew members, so you could find yourself paying from £470 (US$700) to £1500 (US$2400) per person per month to cruise. This is usually negotiated in US$ and the normal average is US$25-30 a day at the time of writing

There is another important aspect to the cost of cruising: the question of where you are going. For instance, it will cost more to harbour hop or coastal cruise than to make an ocean passage. As an example, but not a quotation of exact cost, an ocean voyage from, say, the west coast of the USA to the South Pacific direct, could be sailed on a yacht with three to four people for £470 (US$700) per person per month. However, the same amount of time spent on a cruise down the Californian coast, stopping in various ports along the way, will cost three to four times as much. Also, this does not take into consideration money you would spend while ashore.

It should be pointed out that for an ocean passage of a month or more the crew members will be expected to pay the money in advance for the expected duration in order to stock up the boat for a long voyage, and similarly, when stocking up the boat before going into an expensive area. Coastal cruising or harbour hopping usually means easier availability of food, and a large purchase before departure is less likely.

The costs of being a crew member will be:

1 The cost of commercial travel to the port at which the yacht is located.
2 The financial arrangements made with the skipper covering the time you will be living on the yacht at sea and in port.
3 The personal equipment, insurance and documents required.
4 Money spent ashore at ports visited while cruising.
5 The cost of commercial travel from where you leave the yacht to your home.

No charge
The most likely way to crew on a cruising yacht for no charge at all is by a trade off of skills needed such as cooking, maintenance, navigating, etc for berth and board, but you will still be liable for your financial requirements to any authorities. Also, positions are available as skipper/caretakers on yachts when owners cannot spare the time to be on board constantly, and need their boats maintained and brought to areas where they choose to join them. They may then leave the boats again to the skipper/caretakers. This could also be a paid job.

Paid crew
The job most often paid for is a delivery skipper. An owner will pay a skipper, and possibly crew, to deliver the boat to another part of the world or to its home port. Racing boats, too, often need to be returned to their home port at the end of a race after the professional racing crew has left. You will have to have suitable qualifications and as already stated, in these situations one is giving up some personal choices and independence.

Carrying money and proof of financial credibility abroad

There are three ways to handle your money needs while sailing: cash, traveller's cheques, and credit cards. Probably the best plan is a combination of all three. For cash and traveller's cheques, consider carrying more than one type of currency depending on where you are going. International rates of exchange can fluctuate by surprising amounts, and it can be a safeguard against this to carry with pounds sterling and US dollars a quota of French francs, Deutschmarks or yen, for example.

If you know for sure where you will be returning home from, you can purchase an open-dated ticket for your return. These are usually good for six months to a year. Another way of dealing with the return ticket/bond problem, if you are unsure of when and from where you will be returning, is to purchase from any major international airline an MCO (Miscellaneous Charges Order), which is a ticket voucher to the value of air travel you desire. It is good from or to any destination and will be honoured by any airline. They are valid for one year, and can be taken to an office of the issuing airline and extended for a further year if this is done before the expiry date. Have it made out to the highest amount you may require; if you don't use the full amount, the balance will be rewritten on to a new MCO for later use; in some cases, the money is refundable. The MCO will be made out in your name and cannot be used by anyone else. There are some special deals offered by some airlines for which it may not be acceptable.

Credit cards, such as American Express, Mastercard and Visa, are accepted in most places around the world and can be used for purchasing travel as well as withdrawing cash in foreign banks. However, credit cards are not acceptable for a bond.

To establish your financial credibility with skippers as well as when applying for visas to foreign countries, it is a good idea to have a letter of credit from your bank.

You should budget for the following items which should be carried with you while cruising:

Passport
International inoculations card, showing injections received
    such as tetanus, typhoid, smallpox, cholera.
Health insurance policy – either your permanent one or a tem-
    porary policy for travelling.
At least twelve passport-sized pictures of yourself.
Letters of reference from any of the following:
    a) Bank Manager
    b) Accountant
    c) Business associate
    d) Professional acquaintance, eg family doctor, lawyer,

church minister.

e) Photocopies of documents or diplomas showing any special skills you have.

To bring these papers with you will help to establish your financial and personal credibility quickly and easily.

Remember that the more you sail and the more experience you acquire, the more valuable you will be as a crew member. Crewing positions will also become easier to arrange and will cost you less. You should ask for a letter of reference from each skipper you have sailed with.

It's not a bad idea to familiarize yourself with which documents the skipper requires and, with appropriate discretion, establish that they exist! Required in the EU are the Certificate of Registry, proof of home port, age of yacht, VAT exemption or payment receipt, and yacht insurance. In respect of the skipper an International Certificate of Competence (ICC) will also be required.

Other European countries are increasingly requiring these documents to be available for inspection. Different rules apply in and out of the EU and it is worth remembering that the Channel Islands, Canary Islands and Malta are not part of the EU.

Not all these documents are required worldwide, and whether they need to be shown depends on the area. Sailing on inland waters requires extra documentation. However, the Certificate of Registry and proof of home port will be required anywhere.

Mail

Receiving mail can be complicated. This is due to uncertain travel schedules, the length of time international mail takes and the availability of reliable holding addresses at which mail can be collected.

It is best to appoint one person at your home base who you will keep informed to the best of your ability as to your movements. Before you leave you should inform everyone who may need to communicate with you of that person's name, address and telephone number. It can be any responsible person – one of the family, solicitor, accountant, bank manager. This way anyone can know your next address and you only have to keep one person up to date. Ask people to number their letters, then you will know if correspondence is missing.

There are three possibilities for holding addresses. The most common one is Poste Restante at any main post office in cities all over the world. They have varying degrees of reliability; some may hold letters for ten days, some for one month, some indefinitely. Most post offices will file your letter alphabetically under your surname, other post offices just keep one bundle for all Poste Restante letters and you will have to search through them all for yours. Generally Poste Restante is adequate – with good timing and luck. They also have a forwarding service.

The next possibility is American Express offices. In most major cities there is an office or an agent for American Express and they will hold mail for their customers, ie people holding American Express cards or traveller's cheques. They issue booklets which list their addresses worldwide and they keep letters for ten days. Each time an additional letter is received for you that one and the previous one will be kept for another ten days. An advantage is that there will also be a telephone number to which people can phone a message, or which you can telephone if you are delayed. They also have a forwarding service.

The last possibility to consider is the consular section of the embassy for your country. Some consular sections will hold mail if you write asking permission in advance, but you *must* write for permission first. Addresses can be obtained from the Foreign Office. Some countries' embassies will not cooperate, however. This is a very reliable method if it is possible, but the disadvantage is that unlike American Express and the post office (which are usually very centrally located) consulates may be located in areas that are difficult to find in a strange city in a foreign country.

In all cases instruct people to write your name clearly and simply, preferably keeping to initials and surname only, otherwise your letter can easily be filed under your Christian name and you may never find it if you are looking for it under your surname. All places will require sight of your passport for identity purposes.

Warn people that the post office is usually over-optimistic about the length of time allowed for delivery – double whatever they say and you will be closer to the actual length of time it may take, treble it if the letter is not going directly from one capital city to another. When sending mail try to have your letter franked and if you must buy stamps, have them cancelled with the official rubber stamp before posting. It is worth numbering your letters too.

Unfortunately, there is no easy solution to the problem of mail and difficulties must be endured unless you are prepared to rely on the telephone, which can also be complicated as well as expensive. The alternative to this is to take advantage of increasing computerization and using the internet for mail. Most cities have internet cafes now but in more remote places you will find access for a small fee in private houses by asking around.

If you can't find anyone who will coordinate mail for you check out services available at a Mallorcan based company: Website: www.nautimail.com, E-mail: info@nautimail.com.

Some skippers might be interested in enrolling with a service like Ship to Shore which will provide a complete administrative service in the UK whilst the skipper is absent. Mail is forwarded as instructed to the yacht and crew members. Crew could reimburse the skipper for their proportion of the mailing service. Ship to Shore is at PO Box 400, Winchester SO22 4RU, United Kingdom. Answerphone and Fax (+) 01962 868642, Email: admin@shiptoshore.co.uk, Website: www.shiptoshore.co.uk.

Job Opportunities

People are often hopeful that they may be able to work during the course of cruising, either by being employed on a yacht or by stopping somewhere and taking a job, but it absolutely cannot be relied on.

Some countries offer better opportunities than others for international cruising yachties, but in general it is very difficult due to the growing requirements worldwide for work visas and permits. This is in order to safeguard jobs for local people and to select people with specific qualifications. For cutting through the paperwork the best qualifications are in the medical, electronic, and engineering fields. However you will be expected to take a contract for at least six months to a year in most cases. At the other end of the scale, hotels, restaurants, bars and timeshare projects offer opportunities for work as not too many questions are asked provided you speak the local language and you are prepared to earn very little except from tips and commissions. Nurses, therapists and teachers have the possibility of advertising and working privately. If you are discovered working illegally, you will be deported.

Countries that have suffered from brain drains because of politics, war etc offer the best possibilities as they are more likely to be seeking to replace depleted skills. Up to now South Africa and Hong Kong have provided good opportunities, and possibly New Zealand when looking for a job in a seasonal stop-over. Australians, Canadians, South Africans and New Zealanders can usually pick up work in the UK.

It is hard to get jobs on the spot in third world countries for casual labour as there is plenty of it. People with special skills are usually recruited in their country of origin by the governments concerned. This applies to multinational companies too. A German yachtsman who wanted to stay in Brazil and work was offered a job with a German company with interests there, but he was told he must return to Germany to make his job application.

If you are happy to work on yachts, doing repair, maintenance and refit work in boat yards and marinas there are opportunities almost anywhere there is a concentration of boats. Most people look to the US coast and the Caribbean for work as 'boat bums'. There are opportunities in the Mediterranean on professionally crewed yachts for employment as crew. The Balearic Islands is a good location, also the big 'resort' marinas in Spain and France. There's quite a bit of competition though. Charter companies abound and fleets have to be maintained – it's a matter of luck. The Red Sea area is a growing charter area to consider, but the politics should be taken into account.

Skippering, cooking, crewing either on private yachts or with charter groups is a possibility but you will be expected to have some sort of certificate or letters of recommendation. It is hard work and long hours; it is the clients who are supposed to have the fun! If you are looking for a paid job on yachts explore the possibilities found in the classified ads section of the international yachting magazines before you leave. Some charter companies to try direct are: The Moorings, Sunsail and Mark Warner Resorts, and there are several agencies who specialize in yacht crew placements from professional skippers to stewardesses. As with other jobs it's a matter of luck if you are on the move, but in either case regularly visiting boats on the quays and in the marinas and becoming a familiar face is often the best way. For useful addresses see pages 71-72

Looking for a job takes time so don't wait until you are broke before you start looking – and have a return ticket to get you home if necessary.

Sailing Opportunities

Here are some suggestions you can explore to get sailing experience with commercial and charitable organizations.

Some sailing schools now include a mixed-experience long-distance cruise in their itineraries or the opportunity to participate in a racing event, usually lasting a couple of weeks. As rallies and regattas grow in popularity, it is inevitable that commercially organized rallies are evolving to meet and create demand. The charitable organizations are usually geared towards groups wishing to experience tall ship sailing. Flotilla holidays are a good way to get a feel for crewing – probably the closest you'll get to experiencng sailing with virtual strangers on a private yacht. There are many companies operating in the Mediterranean.

Rally Organizers

World Cruising Club
120 High St, Cowes
Isle of Wight PO31 7AX
Tel: 01983 296060
Fax: 01983 295959
E-mail: mail@worldcruising.com
Website: www.worldcruising.
 com

Blue Water Rallies Ltd
Windsor Cottage
Chedworth, Cheltenham
Glos GL54 4AA
Tel/Fax 01285 720904
Email: pandarally@aol.com
Website: www.yachtrallies.co.uk

Windward Sailing
 Crewing Opportunities
15 Spencer Glade, Ryde
Isle of Wight PO33 3AJ
Tel: 01983 612800
Fax: 01983 612777

Flotilla Holidays

Share-A-Yacht Activity Holidays
48 Canada Road, Cobham
Surrey KT11 2BA
Tel: 01932 867418
Fax: 01932 865179
E-mail: info@activity-
 holiday.co.uk
Website: www.activity-
 holiday.co.uk

Sailing Holidays Ltd
105 Mount Pleasant Road
London NW10 3EH
Tel: 020 8459 8787
Fax: 020 8459 8798
Email: mail@sailingholidays.com
Website: www.sailingholidays.
com

Charities

Sailing Training Association
2A The Hard
Portsmouth PO1 3PT
Tel: 02392 832055
Fax: 02392 815769
E-mail: tallships@sta.org.uk
Website: www.sta.org.uk

Ocean Youth Trust
OYT South, Spur House
1 The Spur, Alverstoke
Gosport PO12 2NA
Tel: 0870 2412252
Fax: 0870 9090230
E-mail: oytsouth@aol.com
Website: www.oyc.org.uk

Also at:
North West Tel: 01516 661664
North East Tel: 0870 2416789
Scotland Tel: 0141 3005511
N. Ireland Tel: 02089 3366776

Jubilee Sailing Trust Ltd
Jubilee Yard, Hazel Road
Woolston
Southampton SO19 7GB
Tel: 02380 449108
Fax: 02380 449145
E-mail: jst@jst.org.uk
Website: www.jst.org.uk

Racing Events

Challenge Business
Meridian House
7 Ocean Way, Ocean Village
Southampton SO14 3TJ
Tel: 02380 715300
Fax: 02380 237111
E-mail: corporatesailing@
challengebusiness-box.com
Website: www.challengebusiness.
com

Sailing as a Profession

You can take specific training for jobs in the sailing world. Since this book was first written the opportunities to live and work on cruising yachts as a profession have expanded significantly.

Along with the expansion has come the paperwork. In February 2002 The IMO (International Maritime Organisation) introduced 'Standards of Training Certification and Watch Keeping for Seafarers' STCW (Yachts), this consists of a course of modules that eventually lead to Master of Yachts Certificate of Competency (Class 4) or MCA (Maritime Coastguard Agency) Class 4 Ticket. The Class 4 ticket is not required for smaller yachts (those under 100ft) but it is essential for those considering sailing as a career and planning to move up to superyachts. To skipper on smaller vessels you can start looking for work with an RYA Yachtmaster Offshore commercially endorsed certificate and progress to the Yachtmaster Ocean commercially endorsed certificate. Anybody who is seriously contemplating positions as crew, or captain as a profession must have the required certification to get anywhere, along with sea experience and properly logged sea miles. The RYA Yachtmaster is now considered the springboard qualification for any position from deckhand upwards on vessels over 100ft (24 metres).

The best way to start off is to take the progression of RYA courses from Competent Crew up to Ocean Yachtmaster with a commercial endorsement, and follow the suggestions given in this book to find crew places on yachts, building up time at sea and experience. Participate in the Rallies and Regattas that are presented later in this book. Begin by finding a job as pontoon staff or steward positions in flotilla and charter companies as mentioned in Job Opportunities. This is a good way to get known in the business whilst you build up your qualifications to be:-

Deckhand
First Mate
Flotilla/Charter Skipper
Delivery Skipper
Superyacht Captain (yachts 100-180ft+)

Or, you may consider being a Sailing Instructor. For this you will have to work up to RYA Yachtmaster Instructor.

Engineers need to work through the STCW & MCA modules to achieve Engineer Officer Certificate of Competency (Yacht).

Chefs and cooks are always required, but appropriate qualifications and experience will be required as well as a sailing background.

In the beginning competition is high. Just finding a place as deckhand means systematically doing the rounds of agencies and classified ads, but walking the quays and marinas where the boats are and getting known, helping out with maintenance jobs to get a break, then proving yourself and showing commitment and loyalty, is the best way to get a position. As already mentioned, presentation, personality and compatibility count for a lot.

Women have a harder time breaking into the professional circuit. They need to try harder than men, and prove they're better, otherwise they tend to get sidetracked into being a stewardess. Even so, take that opportunity and work at getting onto the deck from there once you're on board; it might just be the chance you need.

This is a career to be taken seriously. Building up experience, logging time at sea, getting certificates, and working through the chain of command means you are looking at 5-7 years. The bonus is you are living the lifestyle whilst you are achieving it.

Remuneration will probably be nil to start with, but your living expenses will be covered. At the very top you could earn £90,000+ p.a. Mostly people will be earning £600-£1200 monthly with living expenses, and work is seasonal depending on your location.

There are quite a few establishments running professional courses and job placements in England and abroad now, providing excellent facilities.

For MCA Class 4 & RYA

The United Kingdom Sailing
  Academy - UKSA
Arctic Road, West Cowes
Isle of Wight PO31 7PQ
Tel: 01983 203042/203034
Fax: 01983 295938
E-mail: info@uk-sail.org.uk
Website: www.uk-sail. org.uk

Flying Fish - International
  Training & Adventure
25 Union Road, Cowes
Isle of Wight PO31 7TW
Tel: 01983 280641
Fax: 01983 281821
E-mail: info@flyingfishonline.
  com
Website: www.flyingfishon-
  line.com

Warsash Maritime Centre
Newtown Road, Warsash,
Southampton SO31 9ZL
Tel: 01489 576161
Fax: 01489 573988
Website:
  www.wmc@solent.ac.uk

International Yachtmaster
  Training
910 SE 17th Street, Fort
Lauderdale, Florida 33316,
  USA
Tel: +1 (954) 7797764
Fax +1 (954) 7797165
Email: info@yachtmaster.com
Website: www.yachtmaster.com
UK Tel: 0191 5360891
    Fax: 0191 5360888
Palma de Mallorca
  Tel: +34 (0) 971 799853
  Email:
  palma@yachtmaster.com

For RYA only

Hamble School of Yachting
Professional Training
Mercury Yacht Harbour
Satchell Lane, Hamble
Hants SO31 4HQ
Tel: 02380 452668
Fax: 02380 456687
E-mail: tuition@hamble.co.uk
Website: www.hamble.co.uk

Round Britain Experience
Brixham Marina, Brixham
South Devon TQ5 9BP
Tel: 01803 853843
Fax: 01803 85424
Email: enquiries@roundbritain-experience.com
Website: www.roundbritainexperience.com

General

The British Marine Federation
BMF Training, Marine House
Thorpe Lea Road, Egham
Surrey TW20 8BF
Tel: 01784 473377
Website: www.britishmarine.co.uk

Agencies

Superyacht Services
23 St Davids Road South
Lytham St. Annes
Lancs FY 81TJ
Website: www.yachtcrew-cv.com

The Crew Agency
La Galerie du Port
8 Bd.d'Aguillon
06600 Antibes, France
Tel: +33 (0) 4 93 346464
Fax: +33 (0) 4 93 342122
Email: crew@insull.com
Website: www.insull.com

UKSA – see previous page
Website: www.yachtcareers.com

Elite Crew International Inc
714 SE 17th Street
Fort Lauderdale
Florida 33316 USA
Tel: +1 (954) 522480
Fax: +1 (954) 5224930
Email: placement@elitecrewintl.com
Website: www.elitecrewintl.com

All the places shown in 'Sailing Opportunities' p.67 would also be establishments where professionals are required.

Crewseekers – professional positions (introductions only) for full details and other useful addresses including the RYA see Page 93.

Charter & Resorts

Sunsail Human Resources
The Port House, Port Solent
Portsmouth P06 4TH
Tel: 023 92222308
Email: hr@sunsail.com
Website: www. sunsail

Mark Warner Beach Clubs
   Resorts Recruitment Dept
Tel: 020 77617300
Website: www.markwarner.
   co.uk

The Moorings
Tel: 01227 776677
Website: www.moorings.com

Where the Yachts Are

How they travel seasonally

The first step to being successful in business is to find a need and fill it. Once the need is established, you then need to be in the right place at the right time. This premise is also true and equally applicable to becoming a crew member on a cruising yacht.

Where is the need? The answer to this question raises two more questions: First, where is the cruising yacht? Secondly, when is crew needed?

To find the answers to these questions will require an understanding of world weather patterns and the relative seasons of trade winds and hurricanes. The area concerned is the tropic zone located between the Tropic of Cancer at latitude 23° N and the Tropic of Capricorn at latitude 23° S. Here, during certain parts of the year, the north-east trade winds north of the Equator and the south-east trade winds south of the Equator are found.

It is these east to west blowing, warm trade winds of 10 to 25 knots plus the easy going, happy, relaxed people found on islands and continents in this zone that draw cruising yachts to it. Unfortunately, the tropic zone is also where hurricanes with winds of 65 to 175 knots or more are formed. However, their times and places of origin are fairly well defined. North of the Equator they arise between the months of August and November, and south of the Equator between December and March.

Like the birds, yachts migrate in and out of the tropic zone. Whether yachts are circumnavigating or just cruising around the oceans of the world, they gather at certain points in the tropic zone before making their ocean passages according to these weather patterns. Thus, these are also the places where skippers most need crew. There are a group of people who continue to be undeterred by a circumnavigation from west to east via the

73

'Roaring Forties'. They will normally originate in the summer from Europe or the east coast of America.

The need for crew

You may have decided you want to crew on a yacht, but will a skipper want or need crew? A skipper may be the type of person who enjoys having a crew – and different crews – because it's all part of the experience. Others really don't like having anyone else on board, not even for the sake of a helping hand. There are skippers, couples in particular, who think they might like additional crew, but don't want the bother of strangers on board. Some skippers have had unfortunate experiences with crew in the past and are not willing to take the risk again. Some people plainly see they need crew and tolerate it as a necessity only, but there are also skippers who would love to have crew if only they could find someone suitable.

In order for skippers to get over the hurdles of these feelings about taking on crew, you have to present yourself properly and positively, but without being pushy. Be willing to make a proper commitment to the skipper for the voyage, and be prepared to swing the balance in your favour with a financial incentive to the skipper that may finally tempt him to take you – it's not unusual to pay for experience. Once you get a crew position, and have established yourself as a good crew member, it will be easier to pick up other places on yachts. You will become known by other yacht owners, assessed by them (maybe even recommended), so that if someone is looking for crew your name will automatically come up. It's easier to move from one boat to another than to break into the circuit for the first time, so don't be disheartened if it takes a while to get started.

Underlying this whole situation is a further complication in certain locations. This is the skipper's fear that would-be crew might be potential hijackers planning to use a yacht for drug smuggling. This is of course a real problem, and one to which the skipper always needs to be alert. However, the result is that it becomes hard for people who genuinely want to crew. In the section dealing with socio-cultural issues, we discussed skippers' need to safeguard themselves by preventing illegal drugs being brought on board by crew and how it may affect everyone aboard. Skippers can include a search for weapons, but lack of weapons does not prove anything if people posing as crew are intent on hijacking the yacht once at sea.

In the chapter on financial preparation, we advised the carrying of letters of reference from bank managers, lawyers, doctors, church ministers, etc, so that it will be easier to establish financial and personal credibility. These references, as well as references from skippers you have sailed with previously, will help to reassure a wary skipper, so it is well worth making the effort to obtain them and you should expect them to be followed up. Of course, references cannot be viewed as guarantees by either party, but they will help, combined with the way you present yourself generally.

When looking for yachts to sail on do be cautious: some skippers *are* drug smugglers. It is not a bad idea to talk with other yachties, chandlers, boatyard managers in the same harbour, marina or yacht club about your intention to sail on a certain yacht. You may learn something of interest about the yacht or its skipper that will help you make a decision.

As technology advances, more facilities become available to the cruising skipper and it becomes more feasible to sail with fewer people on board. Commercial shipping is leading the way and, to cut manning costs, 'high tech' electronic equipment and communications perform many of the functions previously carried out by humans. A skeleton crew is required to monitor the automated bridge and there is often no longer a helm. This is not what most yachties are seeking, but there has now come a time when it is possible to go to a yachtbroker and virtually buy a boat off the shelf equipped to go blue-water sailing with little or no experience required, and minimum self-preparation in seamanship.

Satellite navigation systems that can be interfaced with self-steering units, compass course and log, sophisticated radio equipment and self-furling sails add to the ease of manning a boat. Previously, a lot more would have had to be learned about basic seamanship, navigation and helming, and more help would have been needed to make difficult and sometimes risky sail changes.

However, especially since the introduction of huge automated ships, limited in manoeuvrability, restricted more and more to certain shipping lanes and with few human eyes on watch, more care is required by small boats to avoid collisions at sea. Might is right, and yachts are having to sail more defensively, which means having someone on deck at all times. The pressure that this or an emergency situation can put on a skipper with insufficient crew, or on a couple sailing together, will often convince them that additional crew is an essential.

Most people worry about storms at sea when considering an ocean passage; although these do occur, so long as you are sailing in the right areas for the seasons, the risk of encountering storms is minimal. Apart from colliding with large ships, the biggest danger for a boat is land.

More boats are lost when making a landfall than for any other reason. A few mistakes in the open ocean in boat handling or a slight error in navigation won't matter so much, but when closing on land where there is less room for manoeuvre they could be serious. This is the time when a skipper has to be really alert and so does the crew. There will be an increase in shipping traffic of all kinds, especially fishing boats at night. There are reefs, rocks and islands to negotiate, and coming into port requires all hands on deck to look for significant headlands, bays, mountains and navigational buoys. At night, flashing lights have to be located and identified, and their sequences counted properly. Charts have to be continually referred to and, once in a harbour, there is the job of anchoring or finding a suitable mooring, entailing a good deal of rope handling. It is at this period of high activity and concentration that undermanned yachts will often have problems, and these are the circumstances in which crew members play an important part.

An essential part of cruising is the provisioning and preparation of the yacht for a voyage. This is also an important part of the crew's job. When leaving from a home port, much hard work has to be done to a boat to make it shipshape; every part of it has to be overhauled, some items have to be replaced, and often new equipment is bought and installed. Much the same has to be done in ports *en route*, though to a lesser degree, as part of the general maintenance of the yacht. The skipper will expect the crew to assist here too. In fact, it is an excellent opportunity to get to know the yacht, see how things are stowed, and how they work. Moreover, this is the ideal time to get to know the skipper's personality, attitudes and how they work. If you don't get on together, it's not too late to leave!

Finding a crew position along the known yacht routes can often be easier than at the outset of an ocean passage from a home continent, even though it may not be so economical or convenient. The family or friends that skippers set out with often have to return home, or some drama *en route* may have convinced a skipper of the need for crew. There are natural bottlenecks where boats will congregate in numbers while waiting for the weather or the season for the next leg of the voyage. Sometimes they wait for a brief period; sometimes for a few months, as in the case of having to 'hole up' for a hurricane season to pass by. This will be made clearer by the world chart and seasonal calendar on pages 82-89.

It is interesting to note that recent statistics show that Gibraltar has the most cruising boats passing through it at nearly 5000. After that comes Horta, The Azores at about 1,200. Half the boats crossing the Atlantic are bound for the Caribbean, about 500. Australia receives about 800. The Panama Canal, New Zealand, Tahiti and Marquesas have around 500. Then comes Brazil with approximately 300. Galapagos and St Helena receive 150-200. Cape Town and Durban about 100.

Using the seasonal calendar and world chart

With this information you can plan your voyage either:

- To suit the part of the year you have available
- To suit the amount of time you have available
- To sail in the area you desire at the appropriate time

The oceans are listed in an order that follows the migrational movements of the yachts.

By selecting the calendar months in the part of the year you require and then reading through the ocean areas listed vertically, you will see in what areas the yachts are at that time of year.

By reading across the calendar months you can estimate how much time you will require by seeing how many months it takes a yacht to travel from one area to another.

By reading across from the ocean areas in which you wish to sail, you can see what time of year the yachts will be in those areas.

This information will also help you:

1 To decide on leaving from a port in your own country by

77

matching the time of year you can travel with the season of departure for the yachts.

2 To decide to travel to the area you want to be in and arrive at the optimum time for finding a crew position.

3 If you are already travelling or are making other travel arrangements, you can see how a yacht voyage could be incorporated into your plans, or how you could make ocean sailing part of your onward travel plans.

The world chart will help you to see the locations concerned and shows the flow of yacht movements.

Locations and seasonal bottlenecks

The seasonal calendar and world chart on pages 82-89 show where the largest numbers of cruising yachts are located at various times of the year. There are certain places where they will bunch up while waiting for seasonal weather patterns to emerge before moving on. Some other areas are in continual use.

The following locations will be the easiest and best places to make contact with yacht skippers who may need crew.

North Pacific Ocean
South California, Santa Barbara to San Diego in October.

Mexico, Cabo San Lucas and La Paz at Christmas.

Hawaiian Islands, Hilo (Radio Bay), Hawaii, Lahina and Mauii from May to September in all directions.

Ala Wai, Honolulu in August/September for returning TransPac racers to the USA.

Philippines – Liloan, Cebu Island in August/September.

Hong Kong from December to April, all Asian destinations and for yacht deliveries to USA and Europe.

South Pacific Ocean
Tahiti, French Polynesia from April to September/October. Fiji in September.

New Zealand, North Island at Bay of Islands in March.

Panama Canal – South Pacific end, Balboa Yacht Club April/May (Caribbean end, Panama Canal Yacht Club, Cristobal) the Pacific. November for the Caribbean.

Indian Ocean
Australia at Darwin in July/August.
South Africa at Durban in December.
Sri Lanka, Galle in December/January.

South Atlantic Ocean
South Africa at Cape Town in January/February.

North Atlantic Ocean
British and North European ports to the Iberian coast – Lisbon/ Vilamoura from May to August.
(Yachts should have crossed Bay of Biscay by the end of August.)
Bermuda in November and April to August.
The Canary Islands, Las Palmas and Madeira, Funchal in November.
Fort Lauderdale, Florida, in November.

Mediterranean
Gibraltar, Palma, Malta and many other ports from April to November.
November to May cruising yachts 'winter' for the season before cruising again in the following locations:
Turkey: Bodrum, Antalya (Marinas Kemur & Setur).
Cyprus: Lanarca, Limassol.
Tunisia: Monastir.

Note: Apart from some diving charters in the Red Sea area, there is very little cruising traffic to rely on from the Mediterranean into the Indian Ocean. An inconvenient passage combined with a difficult political area reduces the flow of yachts going south. In the opposite direction, more yachts go via the Suez Canal as a convenient short cut back to Europe from the Indian Ocean – despite the inconveniences – if they do not wish to go round Africa.

Caribbean
St Thomas, Virgin Islands in November.
St Lucia, Barbados, Grenada in November/December.
Panama Canal – Caribbean end Panama Canal Yacht Club, Cristobal in April/May (South Pacific end, Balboa Yacht Club) for the Pacific. November for the Caribbean.

Rallies and regattas

These annual events are growing in popularity for cruising yachts. Rallies provide a framework that eases bureaucracy and forward planning, they offer a competitive element, and the security of travelling with other yachts especially in remote or politically insecure areas.

There are several regattas that cruising boats are attracted to around the world, as they provide some light-hearted entertainment and socializing within the cruising calendar.

▲ Around the World Cruising Rally (biennial)
October – Section 1 *Rally Antigua*: Gibraltar, Tenerife, Caribbean. Panama, Galapagos, French Polynesia, Tonga, Fiji to Cairns & Darwin.
Aug/Sept – Section 2 *Oz/Med Rally*: Australia, Indonesia, Singapore, Phuket, Sri Lanka, Maldives, Djibouti, Suez, Mediterranean to Gibraltar. (Part-sections available.)

∗ ABC Rally (Atlantic-Brazil Cruise)
November – Las Palmas, Gran Canaria via Cape Verde Is. to Salvador.

∗ ARC Rally (Atlantic Rally for Cruisers)
November – Las Palmas, Gran Canaria to Rodney Bay, St Lucia.

■ Governor's Cup Race (biennial)
5th December – Cape Town to St Helena.

■▲ King's Cup Regatta
Phuket, Thailand. One week of day racing and socializing held in honour of the King's birthday on 5th December. Attended by most cruising yachts in the area. Website: www.sail-thailand.com

●■ La Source Festival
January/February – St George, Grenada.Website: www.grenadasailingfestival.com & www.interknowledge.com/grenada/gdcd01.htm

■ Antigua Sailing Week/Caribbean Regatta
April/May – Guadeloupe, Antigua BVI. Website: www.interknowledge.com/antigua-barbuda/agsail01.htm

- Angostura Yachting World Regatta: May – Tobago.

* ARC Europe
  May – Antigua and St Augustine, Florida to Bermuda, Azores, Lagos, Plymouth.

■◆ Eastern Mediterranean Rally
  May – Turkey to Egypt. Annual variations of route, but generally including Istanbul, Antalya, Boyzaki, Girne, Cyprus, Haifa, Tel Aviv, Alexandria. Main starting point is Setur Marina, Antalya. Local contact: Kemer Marina, Antalya.

■◆ St Petersburg 2003 Celebration Rally
  – from European destinations arriving in May. Local contact: Email: vliv@medport.ru, Mr Vladimir Ivankiv

* Rally Portugal
  June – Plymouth, Bayona, Viana do Costelo, Lisbon, Lagos.

■◆ Blue Onega Festival Rally
  July – St Petersburg, Petrozavodsk, Lake Onega.Local contact: Email: vliv@medport.ru, Mr Vladimir Ivankiv

* Classic Malts Cruise
  July – 2 weeks around Isles of Oban, Sky, Islay and distilleries

▲ Biscay Triangle
  July/Aug – 3 weeks Torquay, La Coruna (Spain), La Trinite (Brittany), Torquay.

■◆ Black Sea Rally
  August – Atakoy Marina, Istanbul; coastal tour to Samsun and return. Fax: 00 90 212 5607270

The following symbols show who either organizes these events or who will have up-to-date information.

* World Cruising Club

◆ Cruising Association

▲ Blue Water Rallies/Windward Sailing

■ Local information, Marina, Tourist Board, Appendix 2

- Trinidad & Tobago Yachting Association
  Tel/Fax: (001) 868 634 4376

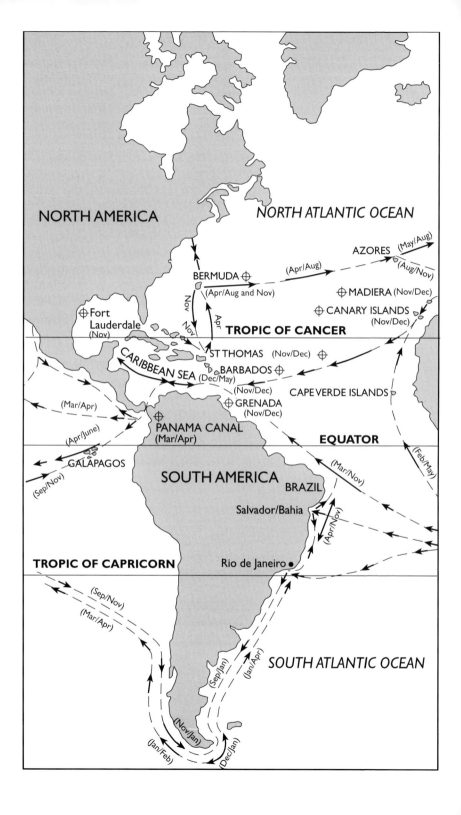

NORTH AMERICA

NORTH ATLANTIC OCEAN

AZORES (May/Aug)

(Apr/Aug)

(Aug/Nov)

BERMUDA ⊕

MADIERA (Nov/Dec)

(Apr/Aug and Nov)

⊕ CANARY ISLANDS

⊕ Fort
Lauderdale
(Nov)

Nov

Apr

TROPIC OF CANCER

(Nov/Dec)

Nov

ST THOMAS   (Nov/Dec) ⊕

CARIBBEAN SEA

BARBADOS ⊕

(Dec/May)

(Nov/Dec)

CAPE VERDE ISLANDS

(Mar/Apr)

⊕ GRENADA
(Nov/Dec)

(Apr/June)

⊕
PANAMA CANAL
(Mar/Apr)

EQUATOR

(Feb/May)

(Sep/Nov)

GALAPAGOS

SOUTH AMERICA

BRAZIL

(Mar/Nov)

Salvador/Bahia

(Apr/Nov)

TROPIC OF CAPRICORN

Rio de Janeiro ●

(Sep/Nov)

SOUTH ATLANTIC OCEAN

(Mar/Apr)

(Sep/Jan)

(Jan/Apr)

(Nov/Jan)

(Jan/Feb)

(Dec/Jan)

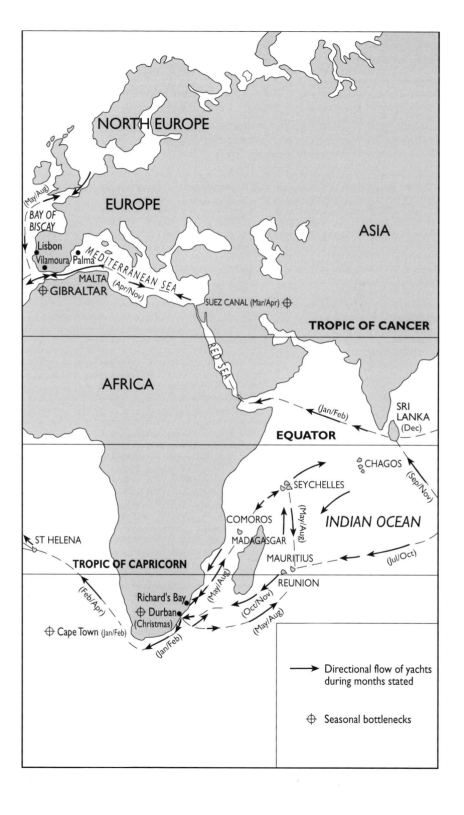

NORTH EUROPE

EUROPE

ASIA

(May/Aug)

BAY OF
BISCAY

Lisbon
Vilamoura Palma
MALTA
⊕ GIBRALTAR

MEDITERRANEAN SEA

(Apr/Nov)

SUEZ CANAL (Mar/Apr) ⊕

TROPIC OF CANCER

AFRICA

RED SEA

(Jan/Feb)

SRI
LANKA
(Dec)

EQUATOR

CHAGOS

SEYCHELLES

(Sep/Nov)

COMOROS

MADAGASGAR

(May/Aug)

INDIAN OCEAN

MAURITIUS

(Jul/Oct)

ST HELENA

TROPIC OF CAPRICORN

REUNION

(Feb/Apr)

Richard's Bay

(May/Aug)

(Oct/Nov)

⊕ Durban
(Christmas)

(May/Aug)

⊕ Cape Town (Jan/Feb)

(Jan/Feb)

⟶ Directional flow of yachts
       during months stated

⊕   Seasonal bottlenecks

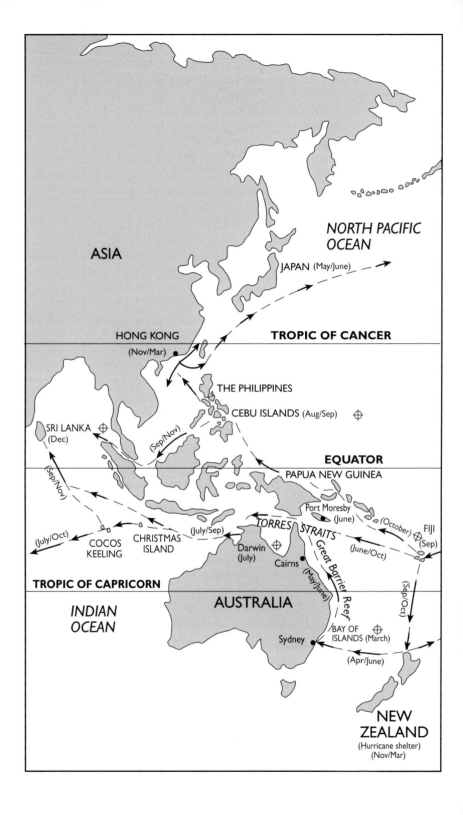

ASIA

NORTH PACIFIC
OCEAN

JAPAN (May/June)

HONG KONG
(Nov/Mar)

TROPIC OF CANCER

THE PHILIPPINES

CEBU ISLANDS (Aug/Sep)

SRI LANKA
(Dec)

(Sep/Nov)

EQUATOR

PAPUA NEW GUINEA

(Sep/Nov)

Port Moresby
(June)

(October)

FIJI
(Sep)

(July/Oct)

(July/Sep)

TORRES STRAITS

Darwin
(July)

(June/Oct)

COCOS
KEELING

CHRISTMAS
ISLAND

Cairns

Great Barrier Reef

(May/June)

(Sep/Oct)

TROPIC OF CAPRICORN

INDIAN
OCEAN

AUSTRALIA

BAY OF
ISLANDS (March)

Sydney

(Apr/June)

NEW
ZEALAND
(Hurricane shelter)
(Nov/Mar)

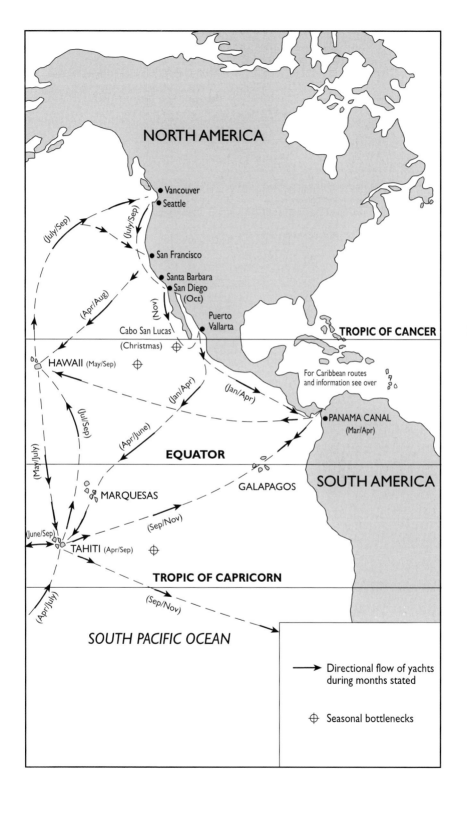

	JANUARY	FEBRUARY	MARCH
NORTH PACIFIC	**Mexico** going South **Philippines, Hong Kong** going to **Japan, USA, Singapore**	**Mexico, Costa Rica, Panama** going South **Philippines, Hong Kong** going to **Japan, USA, Singapore**	**Mexico, Costa Rica, Panama** departing for **USA (W Coast)** via **Hawaii** or **South Pacific Tahiti** and on to **New Zealand** **USA** (S California) departing for **South Pacific, Tahiti, Philippines, Hong Kong** departing for **Japan, USA**
SOUTHPACIFIC	*Hurricane Season*	*Hurricane Season*	*Hurricane Season* **New Zealand** preparing to go to **Australia, Papua New Guinea, USA** (W Coast) via **Hawaii** and East via **Pacific Islands**
INDIAN OCEAN	**Sri Lanka** (Galle) departing for **Red Sea, Suez Canal** *Southern Cyclone Season* **South Africa** (Richard's Bay, Durban) departing for Cape Town and **Atlantic**	**Sri Lanka** departing for Red Sea, Suez Canal *Southern Cyclone Season* **South Africa** (Richard's Bay, Durban) departing for Cape Town and Atlantic	**Suez Canal** arriving from **Red Sea** to **Mediterranean** *Southern Cyclone Season*
SOUTH ATLANTIC	**Cape Town** to **South America, Caribbean, Mediterranean** **Cape Horn** going West and East	**Cape Town** to **South America, Caribbean, Mediterranean** **Cape Horn, Chile** to **Pacific, Argentina** to **Atlantic**	**South Africa** (Cape Town) departing for **South America, Caribbean, Europe, Mediterranean** **Panama Canal** to **Pacific**
NORTH ATLANTIC	*Winter and Caribbean Season*	*Winter and Caribbean Season*	*Winter and Caribbean Season*
MEDITERRANEAN	*Winter Season*	*Winter Season*	*Winter Season*
CARIBBEAN	All islands	All islands	**All islands** going North for **USA** (E Coast) via **Bermuda** or to **Mediterranean**. Also going South to **Panama Canal** **Panama Canal** coming from **South America, Caribbean** to **South Pacific, Tahiti, Hawaii, USA (W Coast)**

APRIL	MAY	JUNE	
Mexico, Costa Rica, Panama departing for USA (W Coast), Hawaii or South Pacific, Tahiti and on to New Zealand USA (S California) deoarting for Hawaii, South Pacific, Tahiti and on to New Zealand	USA (S California) departing for Hawaii or South Pacific, Tahiti and on to New Zealand Hawaii departing for Pacific, Marquesas, Tahiti *N W Typhoon Season*	USA (S California) departing for Hawaii or South Pacific, Tahiti and on to New Zealand Hawaii to All Destinations *N W Typhoon Season:* sheltering at Liloan, Cebu Island, Philippines	NORTH PACIFIC
New Zealand leaving for Australia, Papua New Guinea, USA (W Coast) via Hawaii and East via Pacific Islands	Cruising in: Australia (Sydney, Cairns, Barrier Reef) Melanesia (Vanuata, Fiji, Solomons, Papue New Guinea) Marquessa, French Polynesia	Papua New Guinea (Port Moresby) leaving for Torres Straits, Bali, Indonesia and Australia (Darwin) to Indian Ocean South Pacific, Tahiti going North, West and East	SOUTHPACIFIC
Suez Canal arriving from Red Sea to Mediterranean *Southern Cyclone Season*	South Africa (Durban) departing for Comoros, Seychelles, Chagos or Mauritius, Reunion	Australia departing for Bali, Indonesia and Indian Ocean Islands South Africa (Durban) departing for Indian Ocean to Comoros, Chagos, Seychelles or Mauritius, Reunion	INDIAN OCEAN
South American Coast (Venezuela, Brazil) or South Caribbean (Tobago, Grenada) Panama Canal to Pacific	South American Coast (Venezuela, Brazil) or South Caribbean (Tobago, Grenada) Panama Canal to Pacific	South American Coast (Salvador/Bahia, Brazil)	SOUTH ATLANTIC
USA (E Coast) departing for Mediterranean or Bermuda	USA (E Coast) departing for Mediterranean via Bermuda North Europe departing for Caribbean, USA (E Coast) or Mediterranean	USA (E Coast) departing for Mediterranean via Bermuda North Europe departing for Caribbean, USA (E Coast) or Mediterranean	NORTH ATLANTIC
Europe departing for Mediterranean, Greece or Bermuda, USA (E Coast)	Europe departing for Sardinia, North Africa or Bermuda, USA (E Coast) All Destinations via Gibraltar, Malta, Palma *Greek Islands Season*	All Destinations via Gibraltar, Malta, Palma *Greek Islands Season*	MEDITERRANEAN
All Islands going North for USA (E Coast) or to Mediterranean via Bermuda. Also going South to Panama Canal Panama Canal coming from South America, Caribbean to South Pacific, Tahiti, Hawaii, USA (W Coast)	All Islands going North for USA (E Coast) and Mediterranean via Bermuda. Also going South to Panama Canal Panama Canal coming from South America, Caribbean to South Pacific, Tahiti, Hawaii, USA (W Coast)	*Hurricane Season*	CARIBBEAN

	JULY	AUGUST	SEPTEMBER
NORTH PACIFIC	Mexico (N W Coast) departing for S California and Hawaii or South Pacific, Tahiti and on to New Zealand Hawaii to All Destinations N W Typhoon Season	Hawaii departing for USA (W Coast) USA (N W Coast) departing for S California and on to Mexico or Hawaii N W Typhoon Season	Hawaii leaving for USA (W Coast) USA (N W Coast) departing for S California and on to Mexico N W Typhoon Season preparing to leave
SOUTHPACIFIC	Papua New Guinea (Port Moresby) leaving for Torres Straits, Bali, Indonesia and Australia (Darwin) to Indian Ocean Tahiti departing for Hawaii, USA (W Coast) or Samoa, Tonga, Fiji, New Zealand or going East	Papua New Guinea (Port Moresby) leaving for Torres Straits, Bali, Indonesia and Australia (Darwin) to Indian Ocean Tahiti departing for Hawaii, USA (W Coast) or Samoa, Tonga, Fiji, New Zealand or going East	Tahiti departing for Hawaii, or Samoa, Tonga, Fiji, Papua New Guinea, New Zealand or East to South America and Caribbean
INDIAN OCEAN	Australia (Darwin) departing for Bali, Indonesia and Indian Ocean Islands South Africa (Durban) departing for Indian Ocean to Comoros, Seychelles, Chagos or Mauritius, Reunion	Australia (Darwin) departing for Bali, Indonesia and Indian Ocean Islands	Christmas Island, Cocos Keeling departing for Sri Lanka, Red Sea or Mauritius, Reunion, South Africa
SOUTH ATLANTIC	South American Coast (Salvador/Bahia, Brazil)	South American Coast (Salvador/Bahia, Brazil)	South American Coast (Salvador going North, Rio going South)
NORTH ATLANTIC	North Europe departing for Caribbean, USA (E Coast) or Mediterranean	Iberian Coast to Mediterranean or Madeira, Canary Islands	Iberian Coast to Mediterranean or Madeira, Canary Islands
MEDITERRANEAN	All destinations via Gibraltar, Malta, Palma	All destinations via Gibraltar, Malta, Palma	All destinations via Gibraltar, Malta, Palma Suez Canal Eastbound for North Indian Ocean
CARIBBEAN	*Hurricane Season*	*Hurricane Season*	*Hurricane Season*

OCTOBER	NOVEMBER	DECEMBER	
USA (California: Santa Barbara to San Diego) departing for Mexico (Cabo San Lucas) and South	USA (California: Santa Barbara to San Diego) departing for Mexico (Cabo San Lucas) and South	Mexico (Cabo San Lucas) for Christmas Philippines, Hong Kong departing for Japan, USA, or Singapore	NORTH PACIFIC
N W Typhoon Season	*N W Typhoon Season*		
Liloan, Cebu Island, Philippines departing for Singapore, Sri Lanka	Liloan, Cebu Island, Philippines departing for Singapore, Sri Lanka or Hong Kong, Japan		
Fiji departing for New Zealand, Papua New Guinea and on to Far East	New Zealand, Papua New Guinea	*Hurricane Season*	SOUTHPACIFIC
	Hurricane Shelters		
Christmas Island, Cocos Keeling departing for Sri Lanka, Red Sea Mauritius, Reunion departing for South Africa (Richard's Bay, Durban)	*Southern Cyclone Season* Mauritius, Reunion departing for and arriving in South Africa (Richard's Bay, Durban)	Sri Lanka (Galle) departing for Red Sea, Suez Canal *Southern Cyclone Season* South Africa (Richard's Bay, Durban) for Christmas and on to South Africa (Cape Town)	INDIAN OCEAN
South American Coast to Tobago, Grenada Uruguay going South	Venezuela to Tobago, Grenada Argentina going South	Venezuela to Caribbean Cape Horn going East and West	SOUTH ATLANTIC
Iberian Coast to Mediterranean or Madeira, Canary Islands for Caribbean	USA (N E Coast) departing for Caribbean via Bermuda USA (Fort Lauderdale) departing for St Thomas, Virgin Islands and Caribbean Canary Islands departing for South Caribbean	Canary Islands departing for South Caribbean	NORTH ATLANTIC
Malta, Palma, Gibraltar Westbound for Canary Islands and Caribbean	Gibraltar Westbound for Canary Islands and Caribbean	*Winter Season*	MEDITERRANEAN
Hurricane Season	USA (Fort Lauderdale), St Thomas going South	St Thomas going South Barbados going North	CARIBBEAN

How to Contact Skippers and Yachties

Now that you have prepared yourself by:

- acquiring some of the skills needed
- having a good idea of what to expect of skipper and yacht
- knowing what you can live with in social terms
- being aware of the financial commitments necessary
- deciding on the time of year, time available and desired location

how do you make contact with a skipper that needs you? There are three basic ways: personal presentation on location, classified advertisements, and yacht clubs and cruising associations.

Personal presentation

This requires being where the yachts are. In most harbours, yachties will have a favourite place to gather and spend time socially. It may be the local yacht club, a hotel, bar or restaurant near the anchorage. These are the best places to get acquainted, and most yachties are friendly and will respond if asked where they are from and how long they have been sailing. You can then reveal your desires and where you can be contacted.

You can also advertise yourself by putting a notice on a bulletin board. Normally, all yacht clubs have one, so do marina offices and shops. The nearest laundrette to the harbour is a good place to put up a notice as they are one of the first places yachties will go to on arriving in port, along with the Poste Restante counter at the Post Office. Consider putting up notices at boatyards and drydocks too; all these areas are the natural habitat of cruisers on shore.

A good advertisement for a notice board should include:

Nationality
Sex
Age
Photo
Crewing experience
Skills
Date available and length of time
Desired destination
Financial arrangements – willingly discussed
Place/address where you can be contacted
Date the advertisement

Once you have placed your notices and possibly had the opportunity to see where the yachties socialize and have talked to one or two, your next source of contact will be through the yachties' grapevine.

In any place where there is a congregation of boats there will be a communication grapevine among the yachties as they constantly exchange information whenever they get together. In some harbours where larger numbers of yachts are gathered, there will often be a daily VHF radio session at a prearranged time and channel, called a 'net', organized by one of the yachties in the harbour. Yachts tune in to answer a roll call and have the opportunity to announce any emergency needs they may have. General information is exchanged on the local area and individual needs are aired – and maybe the fact that there is someone in town looking for a crew position.

If you want to experience how this can work, I suggest that you go to Hamble Village (Hamble-le-Rice) near Southampton during the season, when international and local boats are crossing the Atlantic or leaving for other destinations, and you will see how the people in the post office, the pubs and the local facilities provide opportunities, notice boards and contact points for transient sailors. One place that would be worth visiting is The King and Queen pub.

Classified advertisements

You will be able to check the advertisements in the yachting magazines from your home. When answering, you will need to include the same information as you would place in your notice board advertisement – and remember to ask your most important questions. Give your details honestly and, if correspondence progresses, ask the skipper for references and details of experience and who else will be going. Be sure to understand the financial arrangements. If sharing expenses is the agreement, find out what the expenses include. Remember to try to find out whether the skipper is a 'racing type' or whether a more relaxed approach is preferred. Make arrangements to meet and see the boat before committing yourself.

When you do arrange a meeting, it is as well to find out whether you have any other interests in common with the skipper apart from sailing. Notice the person's appearance, and the condition of the boat – generally well cared for and orderly, or disorganized and in need of attention? Discuss and go over navigation systems and emergency equipment. A tour of the yacht will allow you to assess the amenities, your 'space' and to re-establish what is expected of you (duties, finances) and what your important criteria are (food, smoking, etc). In the end, compatibility will be the important deciding factor.

Yacht clubs and cruising associations

This is also a step that can be taken from your home base. Most yacht clubs display crew advertisements. Ask the Secretary to display yours. Choose clubs that have a cross-section of interests which include cruising as well as racing members. Use more than one club. There are cruising associations that will hold registers for crew seeking positions and skippers requiring crew. The same requirements apply as for classified advertisements.

To join crew registers from some of the following sources, a membership or fee is sometimes required:

Cruising Association
C A House
1 Northey St
Limehouse Basin
London E14 8BT
Tel: 0207 537 2828
Fax: 0207 537 2266
E-mail: office@cruising.org.uk
Website: www.cruising-associa-
tion.com, www.cruising.org.uk

Crewseekers
Hawthorne House
Hawthorne Lane
Sarisbury Green
Southampton, Hants SO31 7BD
Tel/Fax: 01489 578319
E-mail: info@crewseekers.co.uk
Website: www.crewseekers.co.uk

Crewing Site –
Website: www.sailcrew.co.uk

The Little Ship Club
Bell Wharf Lane
Upper Thames St
London EC4R 3TB
Tel: 0207 236 7729
Fax: 0207 236 9100
Website: www.little-ship-club.
co.uk

Royal Yachting Association
RYA House
Romsey Road
Eastleigh, Hants SO50 9YA
Tel: 02380 627400
Fax: 02380 629924
E-mail: cruising@rya.org.uk
Website: www.rya.org.uk

Yachting Gateway Ltd
Blackbrook
Skenfrith
Monmouthshire
Email: info@yachtinggateway.
com
Website: www.yachtinggateway.
com

You may find it useful to obtain a publication which lists all the clubs and associations and all the events of the year in the Solent area:

The Solent Year Book
The Isle of Wight County Press
Brannon House
123 Pyle Street
Newport
Isle of Wight PO30 1ST
Tel: 01983 521333
Fax: 01983 527204

Sailors' Thoughts

Maybe a little adversity heightens beauty, for after the storm the sky seemed bluer, the sun warmer, and the sea had a quality of magnificent gentleness. I stood in the companionway for hours, filled with delight at the sparkling ocean and the too blue sky. My uncluttered life was indeed sweet, and it seemed – as it always does – that the simplest pleasures were best.

Hal Roth
Two on a Big Ocean

I would feel an intense depression every time I achieved a great ambition; I had not then discovered that the joy of living comes from action, from making the attempt, from the effort, not from success.

Sir Francis Chichester
The Lonely Sea and the Sky

The mysterious power of oceans to attract human beings is often attributed to our genesis, but why should an ordinary rowboat on an ordinary pond generate similar fears and satisfactions? Depending on our age, the imagination can be stimulated and adventure arrive as the horizon retreats only a few yards, and it becomes quite possible to develop an unashamed affection for the most humble craft. The more sentimental mariners will not think it strange to find themselves in love with an object which floats them upon a special world.

Ernest K Gann
Song of the Sirens

I had resolved on a voyage around the world, and as the wind on the morning of April 24, 1895, was fair, at noon I weighed anchor, set sail and filled away from Boston, where the *Spray* had been moored snugly all winter. A thrilling pulse beat high in me. My step was light on deck in the crisp air. I felt there could be no turning back, and that I was engaging in an adventure the meaning of which I thoroughly understood.

Joshua Slocum
Sailing Alone Around the World

The South Pacific has wonderful therapeutic value, but it has never cured a soul which insisted upon reinfecting itself each day.

James A Michener
Rascals in Paradise

Sailing around the world didn't satisfy our hunger for adventure or freedom, it only sharpened it.

Vicki Corkhuff
SA Yachting magazine RSA

I have been the most happy, the most peacefilled, the most terrified, and the most anxious aboard a small boat, and I think this extreme sense of life is true for most sailors. We pay attention more on the water – our senses are more honed, and if I could zero in on why I like sailing as much as I do as a way of life as well as a sport, it would be for the sense I have of being more alive. It isn't always glorious and blue skies, but at least I know I'm there, and when we are sailing overnight down the coast with the moon full behind the mainsail and it's my watch and I'm alone on deck, I have it all squared away.

Patience Wales
'Cruising through the Magnifying Glass'
SAIL magazine, USA

The tensions and stresses of shore life slipped away, leaving us with the contentment and tranquillity which the manning of a sailing ship at sea always brings. Life was well ordered and we worked the ship between us in regular watches, sharing the more onerous duties. We became very fit, Marilyn also finding relief from her arthritic pains.

Maurice and Marilyn Bailey
Staying Alive

I have been asked many times what it is like to make an ocean passage on a sailboat and what it is about life at sea that draws one to it. The following are some of my thoughts:

You are in the centre of a seven-mile circle and are only affected by what you can see and feel.
It gives one an extreme sense of being.
All of the senses of sight, smell, touch, taste and hearing are acutely brought into play.
It's solitude and tranquillity that engulf one's soul.
It's being warm and contented sitting in the sun without the need of clothing.
It's going from one place to another with just the magic of the wind on the sails.
It's dealing with constant motion; sometimes violent and aggravating, sometimes gentle and tranquil.
It's the aroma of fresh baked bread from the galley.
It's the camaraderie of people helping one another to achieve a common goal.
It's the refreshing freedom of the sea.
For those who are fortunate enough to be in tune with themselves and nature, ocean sailing is the ultimate natural high!

W Clare Davis

I must down to the seas again, to the lonely sea and the sky.
And all I ask is a tall ship and a star to steer her by,
And the wheel's kick and the wind's song and the white
    sails shaking,
And a grey mist on the sea's face and a grey dawn breaking.

I must down the seas again, for the call of the running tide
Is a wild call and a clear call that may not be denied.

I must down to the seas again, to the vagrant gypsy life,

To the gull's way and the whale's way where the wind's like
a whetted knife;
And all I ask is a merry yarn from a laughing fellow-rover,
And a quiet sleep and a sweet dream when the long trick's
over.

John Masefield
Sea-Fever

There are disadvantages to reading too much and thinking too
much and analyzing too much. Everyone must have times when
he is tired and discouraged and doubts the worth of what he is
doing with his life. What matters are not the doubts or even the
opposing justifications. What matters is action. Not to think
about writing, but to write. Not to think about sailing, but to
sail. Not to think about loving, but to love.

Webb Chiles
The Open Boat: Across the Pacific

Sailing along a strange coastline and passing new islands is
always exciting but to do this with perfect weather, sitting out
in the hot sun all day without any need of clothing and with no
schedule to worry about, complete in the knowledge that time is
of no importance, this to me is perfection.

John Guzzwell
Trekka Round the World

Have you ever wondered why so many sail alone? Perhaps they
could not find a suitable shipmate.
Compatibility is the major problem. It is abnormal for two or
three men to isolate themselves from society completely. It seems
very idealistic, on the surface. The romantic adventurer forgets
to consider vital social problems that are bound to arise. Two
men living intimately for such a long period of time are under
much more trying conditions than in ordinary life, they have
ventured out on their cruise to free themselves of our complicated artificial civilization. Immediately they find that there
must be a studied equalization of energies, and a tactful restraint

of personalities. Emotions must be held in check. Freedom is soon discovered to be only geographical, unless one sails alone. Cooped together two men cannot fail to get to know each other too well when confined in a small boat for weeks and months. In time these two will have thoroughly x-rayed each other's soul, hearing the same voice, the same phrases, seeing the same face, over and over again. One can anticipate what the other is about to say or do. Once this point is reached, friendship is likely to wane, to put it mildly, and seldom can it be revived.

Dwight Long
Sailing All Seas In The Idle Hour

On night watches, when one spends a lot of time in thought to while away the hours and when the stars are glittering overhead, I've had the thought that yachties must be the most appropriate group of people to be considered for a Space Odyssey.

Here we are, familiar with space for the purposes of navigation using sun, moon and stars, and getting into more and more sophisticated electronic navigational devices. Here we are, living self-sufficient and independent lives cut off from the rest of the world. Self-sufficient in food and water and transport, self-sufficient medically and in any emergency needing repair, self-sufficient for entertainment and social needs. Here we are, mastering the art of living in a confined space and constantly in motion, in a craft designed more for the efficiency of transport than for ease of living, and being contained in time, space and vessel as we cross oceans, prepared to deal with anything they may bring.

These seem to me to be the requirements of 'pioneers' in space when the exodus occurs.

Alison Muir Bennett

Appendix 1
Travel Facts

In order to check up on the latest visa requirements, organize connecting travel and travel insurance, get your inoculations and read up on the areas you are visiting, go to a travel agent that specializes in individual and alternative travel arrangements. Highly recommended in this field and providing all these facilities are:

Trailfinders Travel Centres
194 Kensington High St
London W8 7RG

Longhaul
travel   Tel: 020 7938 3939

Visa &
passport   Tel: 020 7938 3848

Travel Clinic Tel: 020 7938 3999

and 215 Kensington High Street
London W8 6BD

Transatlantic
& European Tel: 020 7937 5400

Longhaul
travel   Tel: 020 7938 3366

and 1 Threadneedle Street
London EC2R 8JX

Worldwide
travel   Tel: 020 7628 7628

Visa &
passport   Tel: 020 7628 4567

Centres also in: Birmingham, Bristol, Cambridge, Dublin, Glasgow, Manchester, Newcastle & Australia.

Some other useful addresses are:

Bishop Skinner & Co Ltd
RYA Insurance Brokers
Oakley Crescent
City Road, London EC1V 1NU
Tel: 020 7566 5800
Fax: 020 7608 2171

British Airways Travel Clinics
156 Regent St
London W1
Tel: 020 7439 9584

Bridge the World Travel Centre
45-47 Chalk Farm Road
Camden
London NW1 8AJ
Tel: 020 7911 0900
Fax: 020 7813 3350

and 101 Cheapside, London EC2
Tel: 020 7606 2977
Website: www.british
airways.com/travelclinics

Campbell Irvine Ltd
Travel Insurance Specialists
48 Earls Court Road
London W8 6EJ
Tel: 020 7937 6981
Fax: 020 7938 2250
Email: ci@netcomuk.co.uk

Visa Passport Service
1 St Stephen's Mews
London W2 5QZ
Tel: 020 7229 1262
Fax: 020 7229 7656

For yachting gear and equipment:

Marine Force
Enterprise House, Ocean World
Southampton SO41 3XD
and
320 Vauxhall Bridge Road
London SW1V 1AA
Tel: 020 7828 3900
Fax: 020 7828 3383

Capt O M Watts
7 Dover St, London, W1S 4LD
Tel: 020 7493 4633
Fax: 020 7495 0755

Kelvin Hughes
Kilgraston House
Southampton St
Southampton SO15 2ED
Tel: 02380 634911
Fax: 02380 330014
Email: southampton@kelvin-hughes.co.uk
Website: www.bookharbour.com

If you are flying to meet a yacht you must have a document/ letter from the skipper, addressed 'To Whom It May Concern', for the Immigration Department of the country stating your full name, nationality and passport number, confirming you as a crew member, and giving the yacht name, port of registration and number, with details of your estimated arrival and departure plans and itinerary. It should be signed by the skipper and rubber-stamped with the yacht's stamp and/or written on the yacht's headed notepaper.

This should satisfy most authorities as an onward/exit ticket, but they may still require a cash bond. You may also need this letter in order to be able to purchase a one-way ticket, and for obtaining visas.

Very useful advice can be obtained from the British Foreign Office about exotic countries and those in political turmoil, and it is as well to check up on the locations you have in mind. Contact the Travel Advice Unit, Tel: 020 7008 0232/0233, Website: www.fco.gov.uk for information on travel, health, money, hazards etc. (Foreign Office Tel: 0207 270 1500).

Appendix 2
Addresses of consulates and representatives in London

Please telephone first to check address, office hours and visa requirements.

Algeria: 6 Hyde Park Gate, SW7 5EW.
Tel: 020 7589 6885
Fax: 020 7589 7725
Andaman Islands: see India.
Anguilla: see British Overseas Territories.
Antigua & Barbuda: 15 Thayer St, W1U 3JT.
Tel: 020 7486 7073
Fax: 020 7486 9970
Tourism: 020 7486 7073
Argentina: 27 Three Kings Yard, W1K 4DS.
Tel: 020 7318 1340
Fax: 020 7318 1349
Aruba: see p 107.
Australia: Australia House, Strand, WC2B 4LA.
Tel: 020 7379 4334,
Fax: 020 7240 5333
Info: 0891 600333
Website: www.australia.org.uk
Azores: see Portugal.
Bahamas: 10 Chesterfield St,

W15 5JL.
Tel: 020 7408 4488
Fax: 020 7499 9937
Balearic Islands: see Spain.
Barbados: 1 Great Russell St, WC1B 3NB.
Tel: 020 7631 4975
Fax: 020 7323 6872
Tourism: 020 7631 4975
Belize: 22 Harcourt House, 19 Cavendish Square, W1M 9AD.
Tel: 020 7499 9728
Fax: 020 7491 4139
Bermuda: see British Overseas Territories.
Tourism Tel: 020 7771 7001
Brazil: 6 St Alban's St SW1Y 4SQ.
Tel: 020 7930 9055
Fax: 020 7839 8958
Website: www.brasil.org.uk
British Overseas Territories:
Anguilla, Bermuda, BVI Cayman Is., Faulkland Is., Gibraltar,

Montserrat, Pitcairn Is., St Helena, Turks & Caicos: Counter 41, 1st Floor, Globe House, UK Passport Office, 89 Eccleston Square, SW1 V1PN Tel: 020 7901 2150
British Virgin Islands: Virgin Gorda, Tortola, Jost Van Dyke – see British Overseas Territories. Tel: 020 7901 2150 Tourism Tel: 020 7947 8200
Brunei Darussalam: 19 Belgrave Mews West, SW1X 8HT. Tel: 020 7581 0521 Ex 137 Fax: 020 7590 7822
Burma: see Myanmar.
Canada: 38 Grosvenor Square, W1X 4AA. Tel: 020 7258 6600 Fax: 020 7258 6506 Info: 09068 616644
Canary Islands: see Spain.
Caroline Islands: Trust Territory of the Pacific Islands – see USA.
Cape Verde: see pg XXX
Cayman Islands: see British Overseas Territories. Tourism: 020 7491 7771 Fax: 020 7491 7944
Chile: 12 Devonshire St, W1N 7DS. Tel: 020 7580 1023 Fax: 020 7323 4294
China: 49-51 Portland Place, W1B 1QD. Tel: 020 7299 4049 Fax: 020 7636 9756 Info: 09001 880808 Website: www.chinese-embassy. org.uk
Christmas Island: see Australia.
Cocos Keeling Islands: see Australia.

Colombia: 15-19 Great. Titchfield St, W1W 8HZ Tel: 020 7637 9893 Fax: 020 7627 5604
Comoro Islands: see.p.107
Cook Islands: see p 107
Costa Rica: Flat 1, 14 Lancaster Gate, W2 3LH. Tel: 020 7706 8844 Fax: 020 7706 8655
Croatia: 21 Conway Street, W1T 6BN. Tel: 020 7387 1144 Fax: 020 7387 0936 Info Tel: 020 7387 2022
Cuba: 15 Grape St, WC1. Tel: 020 7240 2488 Fax: 020 7836 2602. Tourism: 020 7240 6655.
Cyprus: 93 Park St, W1K 7ET. Tel: 020 7629 5350 Fax: 020 7491 0691 Tourism: 020 7499 8272 Ex 5
Denmark: 55 Sloane St, SW1X 9SR. Tel: 020 7333 0200 Fax: 020 7333 0270
Dominica: 1 Collingham Gardens, SW5 0HW. Tel: 020 7370 5194 Fax: 020 7373 8743 Tourism: 020 8350 1000
Dominican Republic: 139 Inverness Terrace, W2 6JF. Tel: 020 7727 6232 Fax: 020 7727 3693
Easter Island: see Chile.
Ecuador: Flat 3B, 3 Hans Crescent, SW1X 0LS. Tel: 020 7584 2648 Fax: 020 7823 9701 Info: 0906 554 0233
Egypt: 2 Lowndes St,

SW1X 9ET.
Tel: 020 7235 9777
Visas: 0900 188 7777
Tourism: 020 7493 5283
El Salvador: Mayfair House 39
Great Portland St, W1W 7JZ.
Tel: 020 7436 8282
Fax: 020 7436 8181
Fiji: 34 Hyde Park Gate,
SW7 5DN.
Tel: 020 7584 3661
Fax: 020 7584 2838
Finland: 38 Chesham Place,
SW1X 8HW.
Tel: 020 7838 6200
Fax: 020 7235 3680
France: 6A Cromwell Place,
SW7 2EN.
Tel: 020 7073 1200
Fax: 020 7073 1246
Tourism: 0906 824 4123
French Polynesia: Marquesas,
Tuamoto, Gambier, Society
Islands, Tahiti – see France.
French West Indies:
Guadeloupe, Martinique, St
Martin – see France.
Galapagos Islands: see Ecuador.
Germany: 23 Belgrave Square, 1
Chesham Place, SW1X 8PZ.
Tel: 020 7824 1300
Fax: 020 7824 1435
Info: 0906 550 8922
Gibraltar: see British Overseas
Territories.
Tourism: 020 7836 0777
Fax: 020 7240 6612
Greece: 1A Holland Park,
W11 3TP.
Tel: 020 7221 6467
Fax: 020 7243 3202
www.greekembassy.org.uk
Grenada: Queen's St, SW1X

7PH
Tel: 020 7290 2275
Fax: 020 7409 1031
Tourism: 020 7771 7016
Guadeloupe: see France.
Guam: see USA.
Guyana: 3 Palace Court,
Bayswater Road, W2 4LP.
Tel: 020 7229 7684
Fax: 020 7727 9809
Haiti: see p 107.
Hawaiian Islands: Hawaii,
Maui, Oahu, Kauai – see USA.
Honduras: 115 Gloucester
Place, W1U 6JT.
Tel: 020 7486 4880
Fax: 020 7486 4550
Holland: see Netherlands.
Hong Kong: Hong Kong
Tourism Board, 6 Grafton St,
W1S 4EQ.
Tel: 020 7533 7100
Visas: 020 7499 9821
Iceland: 2a Hans St, SW1X OJE
Tel: 020 7259 3999
Fax: 020 7245 9649
India: India House, Aldwych,
WC2B 4NA.
Tel: 020 7836 8484
Fax: 020 7836 4331
Info: 020 7836 2632
Indonesia: 38A Adam's Row,
W1K 2HW.
Info: 020 7499 7661
Fax: 020 7491 4993
Ireland: 106 Brompton Road,
SW3 1JJ
Tel: 020 7225 7700
Fax: 020 7225 7777
Israel: 15a Old Court Place,
W8 4QB.
Tel: 020 7957 9516
Fax: 020 7957 9577

Italy: 38 Eaton Place,
SW1X 8AN.
Tel: 020 7235 9371
Fax: 020 7823 1609
www.embitaly.org.uk
Jamaica: 1–2 Prince Consort Rd,
SW7 2BZ.
Tel: 020 7823 9911
Fax: 020 7589 5154
Tourism: 020 7224 0505
Japan: 101–104 Piccadilly,
W1J 7J1.
Tel: 020 7465 6500
Fax: 020 7491 9348
Info: 020 7465 6500
Fax: 020 7491 9347
Kenya: Kenya House,
45 Portland Place,
W1N 4AS.
Tel: 020 7636 2371
Fax: 020 7323 6717
Tourism Tel: 020 7355 3145
Tourism Fax: 020 7355 3144
Kiribati: see p 107
Laccadive Islands: see India.
Leeward Islands: see Anguilla,
Antigua & Barbuda, British
Virgin Islands, Montserrat, US
Virgin Islands, Guadeloupe, St
Martin, St Kitts & Nevis.
Macau: Government Tourist
Office, 1 Battersea Church Road,
SW11 3LY.
Tel: 020 7771 7006
Fax: 020 7771 7181
www.macautourism.gov.mo
Madagascar: 16 Lanark
Mansions, Pennard Rd, W12
8DT.
Tel: 0208 746 0133
Fax: 0208 746 0134
Madeira: see Portugal.
Malaysia: 57 Trafalgar Square,

WC2N 5DU
Tel: 020 7930 7932
Fax: 020 7930 9015
Tourism: 020 7930 7932
Maldives: 22 Nottingham Place,
W1U 5NJ.
Tel: 020 7224 2135
Fax: 020 7224 2157
Malta: Malta House, 36-38
Piccadilly, W1V 0LD.
Tel: 020 7292 4800
Fax: 020 7734 1880
Tourism Tel: 020 7292 4900
Martinique: see France.
Mauritius: 32/33 Elvaston Place,
SW7 5NW.
Tel: 020 7581 0294
Fax: 020 7823 8437
Tourism: 020 7584 3666
Fax: 020 7225 1135
Mexico: 8 Halkin St,
SW1X 7DW.
Tel: 020 7235 6393
Fax: 020 7235 5480
www.mexicanconsulate.org.uk
Micronesia: Caroline Islands,
Mariana Islands, Marshall
Islands. Trust Territory of the
Pacific Islands – see USA.
Monaco: 4 Cromwell Place,
SW7 2JE.
Tel: 020 7225 2679
Fax: 020 7581 8161
Montserrat: see British Overseas
Territories.
Morocco: 49 Queens Gate
Gardens, SW7 5NE
Tel: 020 7581 5001.
Info: 0906 550 8952
Tourism: 020 7437 0073
Mozambique: 21 Fitzroy
Square, W1T 6EL.
Tel: 020 7383 3800

Fax: 020 7383 3801
Myanmar: 19A Charles St,
Berkeley Square, W1J 5DX.
Tel: 020 7499 8841
Fax: 020 7629 4169
Netherlands: 38 Hyde Park
Gate, SW7 5DP.
Tel: 020 7590 3212
Fax: 020 7581 3458
Netherland Antilles: Aruba,
Curacao, Bonaire, St Marten. See
Netherlands.
New Caledonia: see France.
New Zealand: New Zealand
House, 80 Haymarket, SW1Y
4TQ.
Tel: 020 7930 8422
Fax: 020 7839 4580
Tourism Tel: 020 7930 1662
Tourism Fax: 020 7839 8929
Nicaragua: Suite 31, Vicarage
House, 58-60 Kensington
Church St, W8 4DB.
Tel: 020 7938 2373
Fax: 020 7 937 0952
Nicobar Islands: see India.
Norway: 25 Belgrave Square,
SW1X 8QD.
Tel: 020 7591 5500
Fax: 020 7245 6993
www.norway org.uk
Panama: 40 Hertford St, W1J
7SH.
Tel: 020 7409 2255
Fax: 020 7493 4499
Papua New Guinea:
14 Waterloo Place, SW1Y 4AR.
Tel: 020 7930 0922
Fax: 020 7930 0828
Philippines: 9a Palace Green,
W8 4QE.
Tel: 020 7937 1600
Fax: 020 7937 2925

Tourism: 020 7937 2925
Pitcairn Island: see British
Overseas Territories.
Portugal: Silver City House, 62
Brompton Rd, SW3 1BJ.
Tel: 020 7584 8252
Fax: 020 7581 3085
Tourism: 0903 640 610
Puerto Rico: see USA.
Reunion: see France.
Russian Federation:
5 Kensington Palace Gardens,
W8 4QS.
Tel: 020 7229 3682
Fax: 020 7229 3215
Tourism: 020 7495 7555
**Saint Croix, Saint John & Saint
Thomas:** see United States
Virgin Islands.
Saint Helena: see British
Overseas Territories.
Saint Kitts & Nevis: 10
Kensington Court, W8 5DL
Tel: 020 7460 6500
Fax: 020 7460 6505
Tourism: 020 7376 0881
Saint Lucia: 1 Collingham
Gardens, SW5 0HU
Tel: 020 7370 1905
Tourism: 020 7431 3657
**Saint Vincent & The
Grenadines:**
Tourism: 020 7938 1871
Fax: 020 7937 6570
Samoa (American): see USA.
Samoa (Western): see New
Zealand.
Seychelles: Eros House, 2nd
Floor, 111 Baker St, W1M 1FE.
Tel: 0207 224 1660
Fax: 0207 487 5756
Singapore: 9 Wilton Crecent,
SW1X 8SP.

Tel: 020 7235 8315
Fax: 020 7245 6583
Soloman Islands: see p 107
South Africa: South Africa House,
Trafalgar Square, WC2N 5DP.
Tel: 020 7925 8901
Fax: 020 7451 7284
Tourism Tel: 020 8944 8080
Spain: 20 Draycott Place,
SW3 2RZ.
Tel: 020 7589 8989
Fax: 020 7581 7888
Info: 09001 600 123
Tourism: 020 7486 8077
Fax: 020 7486 8034
Sri Lanka: 13 Hyde Park
Gardens, W2 2LU.
Tel: 020 7262 1841
Fax: 020 7262 7970.
Sweden: 11 Montagu Place,
W1H 2AL.
Tel: 020 7917 6413
Fax: 020 7917 6495
www.swedish-embassy.org.uk
Tanzania United Rep:
43 Hertford St, W1J 7DB.
Tel: 020 7499 8951
Fax: 020 7491 9321
Thailand: 29–30 Queen's Gate,
SW7 5JB.
Tel: 020 7589 2944 Ex 117/118
Fax: 020 7823 7429
Tourism Tel: 020 7499 7679
Tonga: 36 Molyneux St,
W1H 5BQ.
Tel: 020 7724 5828
Fax: 020 7723 9074
Trinidad & Tobago: 42 Belgrave
Square, SW1X 8NT.
Tel: 020 7245 9451
Fax: 020 7823 1065
Tunisia: 29 Prince's Gate,
SW7 1QG.

Fax: 020 7225 2884
Turkey: Rutland Lodge,
Rutland Gardens, SW7 1BW.
Tel: 020 7589 0949 Ex 200
Fax: 020 7584 6235
Tourism: 020 7629 7771
Turks & Caicos: see British
Overseas Territories.
Tourism: 020 8350 1017.
Tuvalu: Tuvalu House, 230
Worple Road, SW20 8RH.
Tel: 020 8879 0985
Fax: 020 8879 0985
United States of America:
5 Upper Grosvenor St, W1A 2JB
Tel: 020 7499 9000
Info: 09061 500 590
United States Virgin Islands:
Power Road Studios,
114 Power Road, W4 5PY
Tel: 020 8994 0978
Fax: 020 8994 0962
Uruguay: 2nd Floor,
140 Brompton Rd, SW3 1HY.
Tel: 020 7589 8735
Fax: 020 7581 9585
Vanuatu: see p 107.
Venezuela: 56 Grafton Way,
W1T 5DL.
Tel: 020 7387 6727
Fax: 020 7383 3253
Vietnam: 12-14 Victoria Road,
W8 5RD.
Tel: 020 7937 3222
Fax: 020 7937 6108
Info: 0906 550 8932
Windward Islands: Dominica,
St Lucia. St Vincent, Grenada..

Appendix 2

Countries without representation in London

Aruba: Arubahuis, RJ Schimmel-Penncklaan, 2517 JN The Hague, The Netherlands.
Tel: 00 31 70 356 6200
Fax: 00 31 70 345 1446
Cook Islands: Principal Immigration Officer, PO Box 473, Avaura, Raratonga, Cook Islands, SW Pacific.
Cape Verde Islands: Mathenesserlaan 326, 3021 HX Rotterdam, The Netherlands.
Tel: 00 31 10 477 8977
Comoro Islands: Brussells
Tel: 00 32 2218 4143
Haiti: 10 Rue Theodule Ribot, 75017 Paris, France.
Tel: 00 33 1 42 12 70 50
Tel: 00 33 1 47 63 47 78
Fax: 00 33 1 42 27 02 05

Kiribati: C/o Office of the President, PO Box 68, Bairiki, Tarawa, Kiribati, SW Pacific.
Netherland Antilles: Antillenhuis, Badhuisweg 175, 2597JP The Hague, The Netherlands.
Tel: 00 31 70 306 6111
Fax: 00 31 70 351 2722
Soloman Islands: Blvd, Saint Michel 28, Box 23, 1040 Brussels.
Tel: 00 32 2 732 7085
Fax: 00 32 2 732 6885
Vanuatu: Department for Foreign Affairs, Port Vila, Vanuatu, SW Pacific.
Tel: 00 678 22347
Fax: 00 678 23142

Appendix 3

Checklist

Passport
Visas
Insurance
Airline tickets/MCOs
Letters of reference/authority
Daily cruising funds
Pocket Money

Hang-out/emergency/escape
    funds
Medicines/vitamins
Harness
Foul weather gear
Personal kit/bedding
Mail/contact arrangements

Are you happy with:

Cruising finances
Yacht insurance/liability/
    documents
Navigational equipment
Safety equipment
Watch arrangements
Cooking arrangements

Domestic duties
Yacht maintenance duties
Food/drink/alcohol/smoking
Your space
Destination
Time schedule
Compatibility

Acknowledgements

Two on a Big Ocean by Hal Roth
W W Norton & Company, Inc

The Lonely Sea and the Sky by
Sir Francis Chichester. Literary
Representative of the Estate of
Sir Francis Chichester. Published
by Hodder & Stoughton Ltd

Song of the Sirens by Ernest K
Gann. Proprietors, Simon &
Schuster, Inc. and reprinted by
permission of the author and the
author's agents, Scott Meredith
Literary Agency, Inc

Sailing Alone Around the World
by Joshua Slocum. Published by
Adlard Coles Nautical

Rascals in Paradise by James A
Michener. Martin Secker &
Warburg Ltd

Article by Vicki Corkhuff in
SA Yachting (Editor, Neil Rusch)

'Cruising through the Magnifying
Glass' by Patience Wales. *SAIL,*
January 1978

Sea-Fever by John Masefield. The
Society of Authors as the literary
representative of the Estate of
John Masefield

Staying Alive by Maurice and
Marilyn Bailey. Random House,
Inc

*The Open Boat: Across the
Pacific* by Webb Chiles. W W
Norton & Company, Inc and
Harold Ober Associates Inc

Trekka Round the World by
John Guzzwell. John Guzzwell
and Grafton Books a division of
the Collins Publishing Group

Sailing All Seas In The Idle Hour
by Dwight Long. Anthony Sheil
Associates Ltd. Published by
Hodder & Stoughton

Note
We recognise with gratitude the important
contribution of Clare Davis to the first edition of this
work.

Index

115

Index